Paris Sweets

For Lesley.
    Wishing you sweet times and a
            Joyeux Noël
                Dorie Greenspan

Broadway Books

New York

Paris Sweets

Great Desserts
from the City's Best Pastry Shops

Dorie Greenspan

Illustrations by Florine Asch

BROADWAY

Broadway Books titles may be purchased for business or promo-
tional use or for special sales. For information, please write to:
Special Markets Department, Random House, Inc.,
1540 Broadway, New York, NY 10036.

B R O A D W A Y   B O O K S and its logo, a letter B bisected on the
diagonal, are trademarks of Broadway Books, a division of
Random House, Inc.

Visit our Web site at www.broadwaybooks.com

Library of Congress Cataloging-in-Publication Data

Greenspan, Dorie.
Paris sweets: great desserts from the city's best pastry
shops/Dorie Greenspan; illustrations by Florine Asch.—1st ed.
p.   cm.
Includes index.
1. Desserts.   I. Title.
TX773 .G698597   2002
641.8'6'094436—dc21

FIRST EDITION

Illustrated by Florine Asch

ISBN 0-7679-0681-0

10   9   8   7   6   5   4   3

To my husband, *Michael*, who made my dream of Paris a reality

To our *Parisian friends*, who make each return to Paris a homecoming

To the city's *pâtissiers*, *boulangers*, *and chocolatiers*,

who make Paris so sweet

And

To our son, *Joshua*, who makes Paris, New York, or anyplace he is

a wonderful place to be

Contents

Acknowledgments

One of the great joys of dividing my life between Paris and New York is that I have twice as many friends and colleagues as I did when I was a sole-city dweller. And for this very Parisian book, I am grateful for the friendship, talent, and help of many *amis, amies, et collègues.*

Among my Paris coterie, I am fortunate to count Patricia Wells as a friend and neighbor. Patricia, the ultimate American food lover in Paris, was the inspiration for this book. It was Patricia who said one evening over dinner, "You should write a book about the pastry shops of Paris." No sooner had she said it than I knew she was right. I have never been happier working on a book than I was while I was working on this one. How wonderful it is to have friends who know you so well.

Without Hélène Samuel I might still be waiting for that first pastry chef to send me the recipe he promised. Hélène, whom I think of as my French sister, and who is much sought after as a restaurant consultant, took time away from her *real* work to organize the Paris side of this project for me. When I started *Paris Sweets,* I thought I could manage it on my own. Now that I've finished— and it is only thanks to Hélène that I met my deadline—I know that it would have been impossible (and not nearly as much fun) without Hélène's friendship, lively intelligence, extraordinary charm, finely honed administrative skills, and unflagging good humor.

I was a great admirer of Florine Asch's watercolors even before I met her and discovered that she is as sweet, sunny, stylish, and chic as her designs. Florine's elegant light touch, her whimsy and wit, and her eye for the romance of Paris can be seen in each of her lyrical paintings. It is a privilege and a great pleasure to have Florine's work in this book.

Martine and Bernard Collet have been our friends for more than twenty years, and it is they who helped us get settled in Paris and they who add immeasurably to our happiness when we are there. A bundle of *gros bisous* and some chocolate kisses, too, for their friendship and their appetites; I think they hold the record for tasting the most "test" sweets.

And thank you to Suzy "Born to Shop" Gershman, a great Paris shopping buddy and an avid test-recipe taster.

Enfin et toujours, there are the pastry chefs, the generous, talented people who make Paris the sweetest place on earth. *Merci infiniment* to the pastry whizzes at Christian Constant, Dalloyau, Fauchon (with special thanks to Sébastien Gaudard), Ladurée, Lenôtre (with special thanks to Gérard Gautheron), La Maison du Chocolat, Maison Kayser, Mariage Frères, Pâtisserie Arnaud Larher, Pâtisserie Lerch, Pâtisserie Mulot, Pierre Hermé Paris, Poilâne, Boulangerie-Pâtisserie Poujauran, Pâtisserie Rollet-Pradier, Pâtisserie Stroher, and Pâtisserie Vandermeersch.

Back in New York, the list is as varied and the thanks as heartfelt.

From the beginning and throughout, this book has been informed by the good sense and good humor of my editor, Jennifer Josephy, who championed it from the first éclair to the last. Jennifer is rare and wonderful in that she is a perfectionist who can laugh, and both perfectionism and laughter are vital in the process of bookmaking.

At Broadway Books, *Paris Sweets* benefited from editorial support from Laura Marshall, and the design talents of Songhee Kim and Umi Kenyon.

And, *encore,* I was fortunate to have Judith Sutton copyedit the manuscript. Judith has worked on all my cookbooks, and each is better for her intelligence and skill.

I was delighted, once again, to have Rica Buxbaum Allanic share my kitchen for recipe testing. Rica's skill with pastry is exceeded only by her grace, energy, and good taste.

Special thanks to La Maison de la France/The French Government Tourist Office, most especially to its director, Robin Massee, as well as to Jana Kravitz and Anne-Laure Trolio for helping to enlist the participation of Paris's most talented pastry chefs; and, once again, a cornucopia of chocolate cakes to Nick Malgieri for his friendship, generosity, and inexhaustible knowledge of baking.

Finally, much love and enormous thanks to my husband, Michael, and our son, Joshua, the two best men in Paris, New York, and all points between and beyond.

$\mathcal{I}$ntroduction

For anyone who loves pastry, Paris is the center of the universe. Not only can you find a pâtisserie or boulangerie on every street, but the odds are tremendously in your favor that you'll find a good, perhaps great, pastry or bread shop, and that it will turn up just when you most need a buttery croissant or a bittersweet chocolate cookie. Like sidewalk cafés, street-corner kiosks, and every famous monument from the Eiffel Tower to Sacré-Coeur, pâtisseries are part of what makes food lovers, bon vivants, and romantics cherish Paris.

Certainly it was part of what made my very first trip to Paris so memorable. My husband, Michael, and I went to Paris in 1971 on a student charter fare. We arrived after twenty hours of delays, long flights, and short hops, with Frommer's *Paris on $5 a Day* and our dreams of what the city would be.

I have many memories of that first day in Paris, among them the lumpy bed and the flowery wallpaper in our small hotel off the rue Dauphine ($4 per night and 25 cents to use the shower), the café au lait drunk on the terrace of Les Deux Magots (and the shock when we got the bill—how would we ever live on $5 a day if coffee cost a buck fifty?), and the endless discussion of what our first dinner in Paris should be, followed by the realization that we had walked around for so long that there was little left open except the corner crêperie (where the spinach and egg crêpe, called a Popeye, was terrific, as was the *bol* of hard cider). These are wonderful memories, the kind that get embroidered into family legend, but they are not as vivid nor as vital to me as the memory of my first bite of a Parisian strawberry tartlet.

The tartlet came from a pâtisserie not far from the hotel. We were wandering the neighborhood, trying to get our bearings, and were drawn to the shop first by the almost overwhelming scent of butter that wafted out onto the street, and then by the jewel-like sweets in the window. To say that that first taste of the two-bite tartlet was revelatory is not to exaggerate. I had grown up on New York neighborhood bakery sweets and I had recently begun to bake at home, but I had never tasted anything like this tiny tart. It was not that it was elaborate; it was just that it was perfect. The deep, rich, absolutely pure flavor of butter permeated the crust, the flavor of vanilla beans saturated the pastry cream, and the baby-sized berries, actually famously delicious *fraises des bois,* were heavily perfumed and so extraordinarily flavorful that they might have served as the model for the ideal strawberry.

For me, the tart epitomized everything that I love in French culture: beauty, precision, pride, good taste, and, most assuredly, pleasure. I was hooked. Hooked on Paris and hooked on the city's sweets. On that trip and on the more than one hundred that followed, I sampled pastries in every corner of Paris, looking for the best sweets the way others search for treasures in the city's flea markets. I would go anywhere for a good pastry—and then I would go again. I developed a list of the best places, what the French would call *les bonnes adresses,* and I shared the list with my friends and with the many people who would call me to ask for tips before they headed off on their own Parisian adventures.

Five years ago, when I moved to Paris as a part-timer—I spend part of each month in Paris, part in New York—life became even sweeter. Not only was I able to have more time in Paris, but I was able to have more sweets—it was so much easier to spread pastries out on a dining-room table than on a hotel bed. Immediately, I took up the practice of *le goûter* (see page 47), indulging in an afternoon snack, and I invited friends to my home to indulge with me and to taste my latest discoveries.

Paris Sweets is a record of thirty years of discoveries. Here you have my best-of-the-best list of pâtisseries and boulangeries, bread shops that offer wonderful simple sweets. You have my picks for what I think is splendid at each shop, as well as stories about the bakers and their wares. You also have something I have never before given, not even to my dearest friends—recipes. Each of the seventeen elite pâtissiers and boulangers featured in *Paris Sweets* opened his files to me and gave me treasured recipes. Most of these recipes have never before appeared in print, in either English or French. In fact, many of them had not even been written out before the pastry chefs scribbled them on small note cards and the odd piece of paper in order to give them to me.

Needless to say, the instant I received a recipe, I rushed home to make it myself. I wanted to be sure that each recipe tasted just as good as the sweets I bought at the shops. Then, when I returned to New York, I prepared the recipes again. The New York tests were the most crucial, because it was in New York that I re-created the Parisian recipes with American butter, flour, sugar, eggs, milk, cream, and even homemade crème fraîche. And it was in New York that I measured out the ingredients in American measuring cups and spoons (eschewed by French bakers, who weigh all their ingredients—even water—and use the metric system), baked them in my American oven, and served them to my very American family and friends. Any recipe that did not taste as good in New York as it did in Paris does not appear in this book. In this sense, every recipe in this book is Proustian, capable of conjuring up with a bite the sweetest souvenirs from the sweetest city.

Paris Sweets is divided into chapters featuring cookies of all sorts; simple cakes, the kind you'll want for *le goûter,* as well as for after-school snacks and after-supper rewards; tarts that are perfect for teatime or, really, for anytime; small pastries and little treats, some as classic as éclairs, others as whimsical as chocolate-striped tiger cakes; and grand gâteaux for parties and special occasions. At the end of each recipe, there is a note from me, "An American in Paris," telling you how I like to serve each sweet, or how I like to play around with it or personalize it.

Dotted throughout *Paris Sweets* are short takes on French ingredients and Parisian customs, as well as stories about each of my favorite pastry shops. It is my hope that these vignettes and anecdotes, along with the introductions to the recipes and, of course, the recipes themselves, will transport you—if just for a moment—to the city I so love.

It is also my hope that serving La Maison du Chocolat's signature tart,

Pierre Hermé's chocolate–chocolate chip cookies, Lenôtre's apple tart with toast points and caramel cream, or Mariage Frère's tea-scented madeleines will bring as much joy to you and your family and friends as they brought to me and to all who have shared these sweets with me. I hope you will grin with delight, as I did, when you make the fresh strawberry marshmallows from the legendary pâtisserie Ladurée; that you will puff with pride, as I did, when you bring Dalloyau's elegant opera cake to the table; and that, whenever you make anything from *Paris Sweets,* whether it is the easy lemon cookies from the jovial André Lerch, the rich little brown-butter financiers from the enormously talented Jean-Luc Poujauran, the soft apple snack cakes from the fourth-generation bread baker Eric Kayser, or, perhaps, the rum-drenched Ali-Babas from Stohrer, Paris's oldest pastry shop, you will be as grateful to the pastry chefs who shared their recipes as I am.

I do not have words enough to thank the chefs for the years of enjoyment their work has brought me and for the happiness they have given me by sharing their recipes with me and allowing me to bring their recipes to you.

Dorie Greenspan
New York City, 2002

Paris Sweets

Cookies

Big and Little, Buttery, Crunchy, Tender, and Crisp

BOULANGERIE POILÂNE

Walk anywhere in Paris, and you'll see small signs hung in café windows that say, *"Ici, pain Poilâne."* "Here, we serve Poilâne bread." It is a point of pride to serve large slices of this traditional rustic bread hewn from distinctive grand rounds, which are correctly named *miches* but have for decades gone by the name *pain Poilâne,* to honor their maker. While you can find *pain Poilâne* in Parisian cafés and supermarkets, it is always worth the journey to go to the boulangerie on rue du Cherche-Midi.

The shop, established in 1932 by Pierre Poilâne, a first-generation baker, and now—and for many years—under the dedicated proprietorship of his son, Lionel, is storybook perfect. The front room, lined with wooden bread racks and filled with the alluring scent of flour and yeast, is a study in browns, each shade a hue found in a loaf of bread. The shop is so beautiful that you might not notice the small back room, an office of sorts. Ask if you can peek, and you'll find it is covered from floor to ceiling with paintings and drawings, each in a different style, but all on the same subject: bread. The first canvas came from a customer, an artist, who paid off his bread bill with a painting. Soon others followed. It is an eclectic collection, topped off, literally, by a chandelier crafted in bread, made for the surrealist Salvador Dalí.

But the heart of the boulangerie is in the vaulted basement, where the breads are fashioned by hand, raised in linen-lined baskets, and baked in the wood-fired brick oven. There is something magical about the space, the heat from the oven, the aroma from the dough, the coolness from the stone walls, and the cloistering embrace of the low arched ceiling.

I remember, with great clarity, the first time, fifteen years ago, that I followed Lionel Poilâne down the worn stone steps to see this centuries-old bakery. That day, M. Poilâne, who is scholarly, encyclopedic, poetic, and passionate on the subject of bread, recounted his beginnings as a baker.

When he was fourteen years old, his father had brought him to the boulangerie and said, "Now you will begin your apprenticeship." The youngster, small and thin, artistic and creative, had known for years that this would be his life, but it was only when it became real that it became unimaginable. "I used to bury myself in the bags of flour in that corner," he said, pointing to where the flour is still kept today, "and cry, trying to keep my sobs from being heard. I did not want to be a baker. I did not want to live underground. I could not bear the thought that this would be my lot for years to come." Then, one day, the young Poilâne had an epiphany. He said, "I opened the oven door, looked into the red-hot hearth, and thought, 'This will either be the door to my prison or the door to the world.'" Anyone who knows that *pain Poilâne* is a household word throughout France and that Lionel Poilâne has established bakeries in Tokyo and London, as well as outlets in the United States, knows what that oven door became.

Considering how devoted Lionel Poilâne is to bread, it borders on surprising to find sweets for sale in his shop. What is not surprising is that the sweets—there are only three: flan, apple tartlets, and butter cookies called Punitions (page 4)—are as exquisitely made as his bread. But then, who would expect anything less from a perfectionist?

Punishments / Punitions

Adapted from Boulangerie Poilâne

Anyone who's ever been to world-renowned bread baker Lionel Poilâne's boulangerie on rue du Cherche-Midi (see page 2) remembers the experience for many reasons, not the least among them the sweet little butter cookies that are there for the taking when you reach the counter. The cookies, piled in a basket and replenished who knows how many times a day, are small and round, with rickrack edges, a pale butter color, and a deep butter flavor. To me, they have always been Proustian: I eat one and immediately remember the butter cookies my maternal grandmother baked every Friday. Given the memories these cookies conjured up for me, I should have guessed that they are, in fact, grandmother cookies. As M. Poilâne explained to me, these plain butter cookies had a special name among the grandmothers who made them in Normandy, his birthplace. There, they were called "punitions," or punishments, and, as Poilâne tells the story, Norman grannies would tuck these sweet cookies behind their backs and, with a smile and a slight tease in their voices, invite the little ones to come take their punishment. Needless to say, the lucky kids never had to be asked twice.

When Lionel Poilâne made these cookies for me in the basement of his shop, he mixed the dough by hand in the time-honored way. He poured the flour onto the marble counter and constructed a wall of flour encircling an empty space, "the fountain," as bakers call it. The sugar went into the fountain, then a small circle of space was created in the center of the sugar, and in went the egg. Using the tips of his fingers, and making sure to keep the flour barrier intact, M. Poilâne worked the sugar and egg together until they were light and smooth. Then he put the butter on the sugar and egg and began working it, too, into the dough, squeezing it in his hand and massaging it into the sweetened egg. Finally, working with the lightest touch, he began bringing the flour into the dough, taking a little of the flour from the inner edge of the fountain's walls and working his way out until all the flour was incorporated and the dough just this side of blended. Watching the dough come together was a lesson in deftness and an opportunity to see forty years of experience compressed into three minutes of work.

For sheer sensuality, nothing matches making dough by hand, but you can make a perfect dough for these cookies in a food processor. In fact, because the

machine works so quickly, it is ideal—use the pulse mechanism and keep your eye on the dough's progress, and you'll achieve the quintessential sandy texture that is the hallmark of these plain cookies.

1. Put the butter in the work bowl of a food processor fitted with the metal blade and process, scraping down the sides of the bowl as needed, until the butter is smooth. Add the sugar and process and scrape until thoroughly blended into the butter. Add the egg and continue to process, scraping the bowl as needed, until the mixture is smooth and satiny. Add the flour all at once, then pulse 10 to 15 times, until the dough forms clumps and curds and looks like streusel.

2. Turn the dough out onto a work surface and gather it into a ball. Divide the ball in half, shape each half into a disk, and wrap the disks in plastic. If you have the time, chill the disks until they are firm, about 4 hours. If you're in a hurry, you can roll the dough out immediately; it will be a little stickier, but fine. *(The dough can be wrapped airtight and refrigerated for up to 4 days or frozen for up to 1 month.)*

3. Position the racks to divide the oven into thirds and preheat the oven to 350°F (180°C). Line two baking sheets with parchment paper.

4. Working with one disk at a time, roll the dough out on a lightly floured surface until it is between ⅛ and ¼ inch (4 and 7 mm) thick. Using a 1½-inch (4-cm) round cookie cutter, cut out as many cookies as you can and place them on the lined sheets, leaving about 1 inch (2.5 cm) space between them. (You can gather the scraps into a disk and chill them, then roll, cut, and bake them later.)

5. Bake the cookies for 8 to 10 minutes, or until they are set but still pale. (If some of the cookies are thinner than others, the thin ones may brown around the edges. M. Poilâne would approve. He'd tell you the spots of color here and there show they are made by hand.) Transfer the cookies to cooling racks to cool to room temperature.

KEEPING: The cookies can be kept in a tin at room temperature for about 5 days or wrapped airtight and frozen for up to 1 month.

AN AMERICAN IN PARIS: To make these cookies even more like my grandmother's, I sometimes brush each cut-out cookie with a little egg wash (1 egg beaten with 1 teaspoon cold water), then sprinkle the tops with sugar, cinnamon sugar, or poppy seeds before baking.

1¼ sticks (5 ounces; 140 grams) unsalted butter, at room temperature

Slightly rounded ½ cup (125 grams) sugar

1 large egg, at room temperature

2 cups (280 grams) all-purpose flour

Korova Cookies / Sablés Korova

Adapted from Pierre Hermé Paris

These easy-to-make, easy-to-eat, easy-to-love chocolate–chocolate chip cookies are from Pierre Hermé (see page 56), the man Vogue *magazine called "The Picasso of Pastry." They are cocoa dark, not very sweet, chock-full of chocolate bits, melt-on-your-tongue buttery, just crumbly enough to be true* sablés, *or sand cookies, and just salty enough to catch you off guard. In fact, the combination of chocolate and salt (Pierre uses the somewhat exotic* fleur de sel, *sea salt from the Guérande; see page 9) makes these cookies fatally appealing: I don't trust myself not to finish the batch in a sitting, and I'll bet you'll find yourself in the same*

spot—a warning to make these when you're certain not to be alone. Indeed, these are the easiest cookies to make for company because, despite their très *French flavor, they are essentially American slice-and-bake icebox cookies. The dough is mixed in a flash, rolled into logs, and chilled, then cut into rounds and baked in minutes.*

*   **About the name:** *Korova was the name of the milk bar in Stanley Kubrick's classic film,* A Clockwork Orange. *It was also the name of a restaurant off the Champs-Élysées for which Pierre Hermé created these cookies. The restaurant is gone, but the cookies are still a specialty at Pierre's pâtisserie as well as the house cookies at my house.*

1. Sift the flour, cocoa, and baking soda together and keep close at hand. Put the butter in the bowl of a mixer fitted with the paddle attachment and beat on medium speed until the butter is soft and creamy. (Alternatively, you can do this and all subsequent steps by hand, working with a sturdy rubber spatula.) Add both sugars, the salt, and vanilla extract and beat for another minute or two. Reduce the mixer speed to low and add the sifted dry ingredients. Mix only until the dry ingredients are incorporated—the dough will look crumbly, and that's just right. For the best texture, you want to work the dough as little as possible once the flour is added. Toss in the chocolate pieces and mix only to incorporate.

2. Turn the dough out onto a smooth work surface and squeeze it so that it sticks together in large clumps. Gather the dough into a ball, divide it in half, and working with one half at a time, shape the dough into logs that are 1½ inches (4 cm) in diameter. (Cookie-dough logs have a way of ending up with hollow centers, so as you're shaping each log, flatten it once or twice and roll it up from one long side to the other, just to make certain you haven't got an air channel.) Wrap the logs in plastic wrap and chill them for at least 2 hours. *(Wrapped air-tight, the logs can be refrigerated for up to 3 days or frozen for 1 month.)*

3. Center a rack in the oven and preheat the oven to 325°F (165°C). Line two baking sheets with parchment paper and keep them close at hand.

4. Working with a sharp thin-bladed knife, slice the logs into rounds that are ½ inch (1.5 cm) thick. (Don't be upset if the rounds break; just squeeze the broken-off bit back onto the cookie.) Place the cookies on the parchment-lined sheets, leaving about 1 inch (2.5 cm) spread space between them.

1¼ cups (175 grams) all-purpose
flour

⅓ cup (30 grams) Dutch-processed
cocoa powder

½ teaspoon baking soda

1 stick plus 3 tablespoons (5½
ounces; 150 grams) unsalted
butter, at room temperature

⅔ cup (120 grams) packed light
brown sugar

¼ cup (50 grams) sugar

½ teaspoon *fleur de sel* (see page 9)
or ¼ teaspoon fine sea salt

1 teaspoon pure vanilla extract

5 ounces (150 grams) bittersweet
chocolate, chopped into small bits

5. Bake only one sheet of cookies at a time, and bake each sheet for 12 minutes. The cookies will not look done, nor will they be firm, but that's just the way they should be. Transfer the baking sheet to a cooling rack and let the cookies stand until they are only just warm or until they reach room temperature—it's your call. Repeat with the second sheet of cookies.

KEEPING: The dough can be made ahead and chilled or frozen. If you've frozen the dough, you needn't defrost it before baking—just slice the logs and bake the cookies 1 minute longer. Packed airtight, baked cookies will keep at room temperature for up to 3 days; they can be frozen for up to 1 month.

AN AMERICAN IN PARIS: In moments of over-the-topness, I've added chopped toasted pecans, plumped currants, and a pinch of cinnamon to the dough and loved it. And, I've been known to cheat on the chocolate bits. On the sad (but fortunately seldom) occasions when my cupboard is bare of Valrhona Guanaja (Pierre's choice for these cookies, and one of my favorite chocolates), I've even used store-bought chocolate chips.

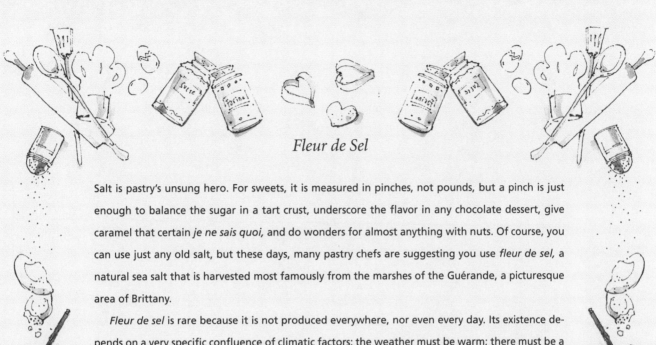

Fleur de Sel

Salt is pastry's unsung hero. For sweets, it is measured in pinches, not pounds, but a pinch is just enough to balance the sugar in a tart crust, underscore the flavor in any chocolate dessert, give caramel that certain *je ne sais quoi,* and do wonders for almost anything with nuts. Of course, you can use just any old salt, but these days, many pastry chefs are suggesting you use *fleur de sel,* a natural sea salt that is harvested most famously from the marshes of the Guérande, a picturesque area of Brittany.

Fleur de sel is rare because it is not produced everywhere, nor even every day. Its existence depends on a very specific confluence of climatic factors: the weather must be warm; there must be a breeze; and there cannot be any rain. When these conditions exist, then the tippy-tippy-topmost crust of salt that forms after a day's evaporation is *fleur de sel.* It is the first salt to be raked from the marshes, and it is raked by hand. Think of it as the saline equivalent of first-pressed extra-virgin olive oil.

Fleur de sel's crystals are much larger and moister than those of table salt or even other sea salt. But what *fleur de sel*'s fans are after are its taste and texture: it is less salty than other salts and its crystals seem to melt more slowly. In fact, if you use *fleur de sel* in something uncooked, like mousse, you get a little crunch each time you hit a crystal.

The only way to appreciate *fleur de sel* is to taste it for yourself (see the Source Guide, page 185), preferably in a side-by-side tasting with table salt, kosher salt, and regular sea salt. If you're won over, you may soon find yourself doing what many Parisian chefs do—carrying a pocket-sized box of it around with you at all times. For sure, you will keep a jar in your kitchen. Put your *fleur de sel* in a tightly sealed container and keep it close at hand; you'll be surprised at how often you'll be pulling tiny pinches from your stash. I say "tiny" because *fleur de sel* is not meant to be used like table or regular sea salt. It is not a salt for boiling pasta or for salting a big pot of soup while it is cooking. It is a seasoning, a condiment, to be used when its taste and texture can really be appreciated. You'll find you get the most from *fleur de sel* in something savory if you use it to finish the dish, to give it its last touch. On the sweet side, *fleur de sel* adds something special to tart dough, to streusel, to mousse, to caramel, and to fruits—wait until you taste it on watermelon.

PÂTISSERIE
ARNAUD LARHER

The rue Caulaincourt is one of those streets that make Montmartre magical. It is at once grand, wide and tree lined, and cozy and bucolic. It is part big-city splendor and part village intimate. Indeed, as much as each quarter of Paris has its own character, Montmartre, hugging the hills at the top of Paris, may be the most individual. Thought of as a small town within a big city, it is home to Sacré-Coeur, the Place du Tertre, where artists gather to paint, and Le Lapin Agile, which Picasso made famous. And it is the rue Caulaincourt that winds through the area, starting at the cemetery at the base of Montmartre, climbing the hill, and, here and there, nestling small terraces where stone staircases lit by iron lanterns descend to the village below, the same staircases Atget photographed so memorably. It is on this beautiful street that Arnaud Larher and his wife, Caroline, recently opened their pâtisserie, a shop that is impossible to miss. It is not just that the scent of warm butter and the aroma of chocolate drift beyond the door; it is that the shop, with its deep red and warm yellow front, its butter-and-burnt-sugar interior, and its lights sparkling off the sweets on display, just about glows.

Actually, Arnaud Larher just about glows too. He is so bright-eyed and animated that his freckles seem to dance on his cheeks when he smiles. And he speaks about baking with such excitement that it would be easy to think he had only just learned to make his first cake. But Arnaud Larher is experienced enough to have been voted France's Pastry Chef of the Year in 2000, and he and his wife have had their own shop for about five years. (Their first shop, Le Péché Mignon, or "The Little Sin," also in Montmartre, was the size of a cream puff and forced Larher into building a repertoire of cakes that wouldn't overwhelm the shop's limited refrigerated space, which may explain why his good-keeping don't-need-to-be-chilled "weekend" cakes are among the best in Paris.) Before setting out on his own, the chef was the chief pastry decorator at Fauchon (see page 128), making all those sugar sculptures and wedding cakes that stop people in their tracks.

These days what stops people at Larher's shop are the little sachets of cookies, including his Croq-Télé (page 14), made to be eaten in front of the television set; his polished chocolate candies; his simple unglazed cakes (these are some of my favorites), among them the Pavé de Montmartre (page 52), a square almond cake wrapped in a golden almond-paste cloak; his tarts, of course; and his almost endless collection of mini versions of his grown-up–sized cakes. Depending on the day, you might find yourself tempted by the Suprême, a chocolate cake filled with a chocolate-blackberry mousse and topped with a crème brûlée made with blackberry tea. Or the Caraïbe, a soft almond cake filled with a light vanilla cream and slices of fresh pineapple. Or the aptly named Extrême, a tri-part chocolate fantasy that separates the chocolate likers from the chocolate lovers. And then there's the classic belle-Hélène turned into a tart. And the macarons (see page 123). And the little savories.

It's not easy to make a decision chez Larher, but it is fun. Not only are you surrounded by dozens of splendid sweets, but stay there long enough and you'll be surrounded by dozens of locals, neighbors who stop in for a hello and a brioche in the morning, and who return later in the day for a little something to tide them over between lunch and teatime or a big something to serve after dinner. If I were new to the neighborhood, I'd make Arnaud Larher my daily haunt. It would be a great place to meet my fellow Montmartrians—at least those with the best taste.

Old-fashioned Almond Cookies /

Amandines à l'Ancienne

Adapted from Pâtisserie Arnaud Larher

At Arnaud Larher's warm and welcoming Montmartre pâtisserie (see page 10), the amandines, a favorite after-school treat, are stacked one on top of another at just about kid height, ready to be quickly snapped up and immediately nibbled. Not that these are kids-only sweets. As satisfying as they are, they are also oddly sophisticated. Here, the simple made-in-a-food-processor batter—a mixture of almonds, sugar, and egg whites—is spooned into small mounds and baked into cookies. But at the pastry shop, the batter is used to fill tartlets, which are then baked just until the filling is puffed and lightly browned. Whether as cookies or tartlets, au naturel or flavored with a little cinnamon, cocoa, or nuts (or even all three together), these pleasantly chewy sweets are ideal with coffee, tea, hot chocolate, or ice cream. In fact, because they are so delightfully plain, they're terrific served alongside a hot fudge sundae or a banana split.

8½ ounces (250 grams) blanched almonds

1 cup (200 grams) sugar

1 teaspoon ground cinnamon, 3 tablespoons (20 grams) unsweetened cocoa powder, and/or ½ cup (50 grams) finely chopped pecans, to flavor (optional)

3 large egg whites, lightly beaten with a fork

1. Position the racks to divide the oven into thirds and preheat the oven to 375°F (190°C). Line two baking sheets with parchment paper and keep them close at hand.

2. Put the almonds and sugar in the work bowl of a food processor fitted with the metal blade and pulse, scraping down the sides of the bowl now and then, until the almonds are finely ground, about 2 minutes. If you are using cinnamon or cocoa, put it in now and pulse to blend. If you are using chopped pecans, wait to add them after all the other ingredients have been added.

3. With the processor running, add the egg whites in a steady stream. Mix about 30 seconds, only until the egg whites are blended into the almonds and sugar— you don't want to incorporate too much air into the batter. Add the pecans, if you are using them, and pulse just to mix.

4. Spoon out a level tablespoon of batter for each cookie, spacing the cookies about 1 inch (2.5 cm) apart on the lined baking sheets. Slide the baking sheets into the oven and bake for 18 to 20 minutes, rotating the sheets front to back and top to bottom at the halfway point. The cookies should puff, firm, and turn

lightly brown around the edges. With a wide metal spatula, carefully lift the cookies off the baking sheets and onto cooling racks to cool to room temperature.

KEEPING: The cookies can be packed airtight and kept for up to 4 days at room temperature.

AN AMERICAN IN PARIS: These cookies are prime sandwich material. You can "glue" them together with anything from raspberry jam to lemon curd, but choco-crazy that I am, I think they're swell sandwiched with the ganache from A Chocolate Tart for Sonia Rykiel (page 66).

TV Snacks / Croq-Télé

Adapted from Pâtisserie Arnaud Larher

Croq is short for the French verb croquer, *"to crunch," and* télé *is the diminutive for "television." Together they form the name of a buttery snack cookie that is made in minutes in a food processor. What legitimizes these as snack food, albeit pretty snazzy snack food, is their pop-'em-in-your-mouth size and their up-front saltiness. I love the idea of a salted cookie, but when I first talked to pâtissier Arnaud Larher (see page 10) about his, I told him the saltiness seemed pretty daring to me. He smiled, shrugged, and said that what was daring to me was only natural to him. As it turns out, M. Larher was brought up in Brittany, which is famed for its rugged coast, its wonderful seafood, and its salted butter. "We used salted butter on our bread in the morning," he explained, "we put it on our vegetables in the evening, and, of course, we baked with it, so our cookies were always salty. I'm just continuing a tradition." M. Larher makes the cookies in two flavors, almond and hazelnut, and packs them together in a cellophane bag tied with a ribbon. I don't know whether or not the regulars who buy these munchables do, in fact, eat them in front of the television, but I do: they're a delicious alternative to popcorn or pretzels on a stay-at-home-and-watch-a-movie night.*

¾ cup (3½ ounces; 100 grams) blanched almonds for almond cookies or ½ cup (75 grams) blanched almonds plus ¼ cup (25 grams) toasted and skinned hazelnuts for almond-hazelnut cookies

½ cup (100 grams) sugar

¼ to ¾ teaspoon salt, according to taste (Attention: ¾ teaspoon salt makes a *really* salty cookie)

1 cup (140 grams) all-purpose flour

7 tablespoons (3½ ounces; 100 grams) cold unsalted butter, cut into 7 pieces

1. Position the racks to divide the oven into thirds and preheat the oven to 350°F (180°C). Line two baking sheets with parchment paper and set them aside.

2. Put the almonds, or the almonds and hazelnuts, sugar, and salt in the work bowl of a food processor fitted with the metal blade and pulse, scraping down the sides of the bowl now and then, until the nuts are finely ground, about 2 minutes. Turn the nut sugar onto a piece of wax paper and keep it close at hand.

3. Put the flour in the work bowl of the food processor and, with the motor running, drop in the pieces of cold butter. As soon as all the pieces are in, switch to pulse mode and pulse just until the mixture looks sandy. Add the nut-sugar mixture and pulse in 3- to 4-second spurts until the dough forms small curds and clumps. Scrape the dough onto a piece of parchment or wax paper. *(The dough can be made ahead, wrapped airtight, and kept frozen for up to 1 month.)*

4. To shape the cookies, pull off small pieces of dough about the size of cherries and squeeze them in your hand to form irregularly shaped chunks. Place the pieces on the lined baking sheets, leaving about ½ inch (1.5 cm) space between them.

5. Bake for 9 to 11 minutes, rotating the sheets top to bottom and front to back after 5 minutes, or until the cookies are set but not really browned. The cookies will still be soft. Let the cookies rest on the baking sheet for 3 minutes, then, using a wide metal spatula, carefully transfer them to racks to cool to room temperature.

KEEPING: The cookies can be kept in an airtight container at room temperature for up to 5 days or frozen for up to 1 month.

AN AMERICAN IN PARIS: To intensify the almond flavor in either the almond or the almond-hazelnut cookies, try toasting the almonds first. Spread the almonds out in a single layer on a rimmed baking sheet and bake for 5 to 10 minutes in a 350°F (180°C) oven, just until they are lightly browned and fragrant. Cool the almonds before grinding them with the sugar.

Financiers

Adapted from Boulangerie-Pâtisserie Poujauran

You can find financiers *in almost any pâtisserie anywhere in Paris, but when you taste these from Jean-Luc Poujauran's charming little boutique on the Left Bank (see page 34), you will understand why connoisseurs travel from arrondissements near and far to fetch them.*

Financiers are as rich as the financiers *for whom they were created and as golden as the precious ingots after which they were modeled. These almond cookies-cum-tea cakes were first made in the late nineteenth century by a pastry chef named Lasne, whose shop was on the rue Saint-Denis, close to the Bourse, Paris's stock exchange. Knowing that his affluent wheeler-dealer clients were discriminating, but also realizing that they were always in a hurry (seemingly a hazard of the job no matter the country or the century), Lasne designed his little unglazed cookie-cake so that it could be eaten on the run sans knife, fork, or spoon and completely without risk to suit, shirt, or tie. I like to think of these as early high-class fast food.*

The original financiers *were baked in small rectangular pans, so that the cookies resembled treasured bars of gold, but the cookies can be—and often are—baked in small boat-shaped molds, and, heretical as it may sound, they can even be made in mini- and not-so-mini-muffin tins. (Obviously, if you change the size of the molds, you'll affect both the yield and the timing—not problems, but points to be considered.) What gives these toothsome treats their defining warm golden color and distinctive rich caramel and nut flavor is* beurre noisette, *sweet butter that is cooked until it turns a deep brown and fills the kitchen with the scent of toasted* noisettes, *or hazelnuts. The batter is quickly made in a saucepan and, because it needs an hour or so to cool in the refrigerator, is perfectly suited to being baked* à la minute, *or to order, whenever a well-dressed stockbroker drops by with a craving for something rich, wonderful, and neat.*

1. Put the butter in a small saucepan and bring it to the boil over medium heat, swirling the pan occasionally. Allow the butter to bubble away until it turns a deep brown, but don't turn your back on the pan—the difference between brown and black is measured in seconds. Pull the pan from the heat and keep it in a warm place.

2. Mix the sugar and almonds together in a large saucepan. Stir in the egg whites, place the pan over low heat, and, stirring constantly with a wooden spoon, heat the mixture until it is runny, slightly white, and hot to the touch, about 2 minutes. Remove the pan from the heat and stir in the flour, then gradually mix in the melted butter. Transfer the batter to a bowl, cover with plastic wrap, pressing it against the surface of the batter to create an airtight seal, and chill for at least 1 hour. *(The batter can be kept covered in the refrigerator for up to 3 days.)*

3. Center a rack in the oven and preheat the oven to 400°F (200°C). Butter 12 rectangular *financier* molds (these were tested in 3¾ x 2 x ⅝-inch [10 x 5 x 1½-cm] rectangular molds that each hold 3 tablespoons), 12 boat-shaped tartlet molds (of similar capacity), or three 12-cup mini-muffin pans, dust the interiors with flour, and tap out the excess. If you're using *financier* or boat molds, place them on a baking sheet for easy transport.

4. Fill each mold almost to the top with batter. Slide the molds into the oven and bake for 12 to 13 minutes, or until the *financiers* are golden, crowned, and springy to the touch. If necessary, run a blunt knife between the cookies and the sides of the pans, then turn the cookies out of their molds and allow them to cool to room temperature right side up on cooling racks.

1½ sticks (6 ounces; 180 grams) unsalted butter

1 cup (200 grams) sugar

1 cup (100 grams) ground blanched almonds

6 large egg whites

⅔ cup (90 grams) all-purpose flour

KEEPING: Although the batter can be kept in the refrigerator for up to 3 days, *financiers* are best enjoyed the day they are baked.

AN AMERICAN IN PARIS: In addition to making these quintessentially Parisian sweets in quintessentially American mini-muffin pans, I often add a little fruit to both the muffins and their ingot-shaped kin. After I've spooned the batter into the molds, I just press a sliver of fresh fruit into the center of each. Plum, peach, mango, raspberry, and apricot are especially good with these buttery little almond sweets.

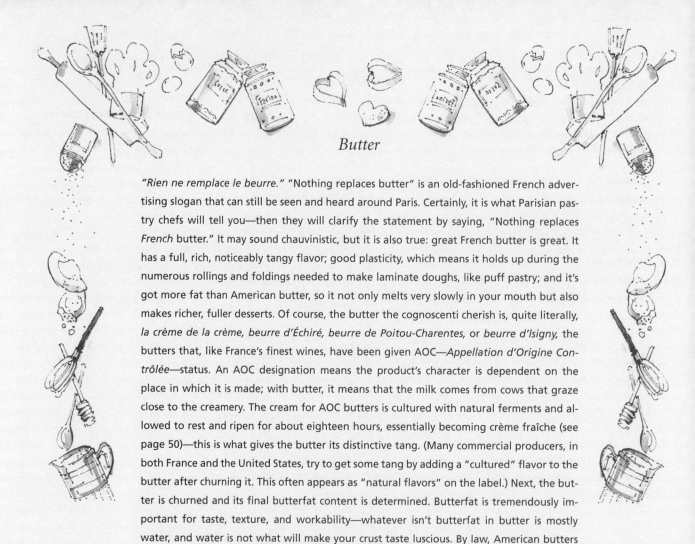

Butter

"Rien ne remplace le beurre." "Nothing replaces butter" is an old-fashioned French advertising slogan that can still be seen and heard around Paris. Certainly, it is what Parisian pastry chefs will tell you—then they will clarify the statement by saying, "Nothing replaces *French* butter." It may sound chauvinistic, but it is also true: great French butter is great. It has a full, rich, noticeably tangy flavor; good plasticity, which means it holds up during the numerous rollings and foldings needed to make laminate doughs, like puff pastry; and it's got more fat than American butter, so it not only melts very slowly in your mouth but also makes richer, fuller desserts. Of course, the butter the cognoscenti cherish is, quite literally, *la crème de la crème, beurre d'Échiré, beurre de Poitou-Charentes,* or *beurre d'Isigny,* the butters that, like France's finest wines, have been given AOC—*Appellation d'Origine Contrôlée*—status. An AOC designation means the product's character is dependent on the place in which it is made; with butter, it means that the milk comes from cows that graze close to the creamery. The cream for AOC butters is cultured with natural ferments and allowed to rest and ripen for about eighteen hours, essentially becoming crème fraîche (see page 50)—this is what gives the butter its distinctive tang. (Many commercial producers, in both France and the United States, try to get some tang by adding a "cultured" flavor to the butter after churning it. This often appears as "natural flavors" on the label.) Next, the butter is churned and its final butterfat content is determined. Butterfat is tremendously important for taste, texture, and workability—whatever isn't butterfat in butter is mostly water, and water is not what will make your crust taste luscious. By law, American butters must contain no less than 80 percent butterfat. In France, the law stipulates a minimum butterfat content of 82 percent. Each percentage point of fat makes a difference, so you can imagine the difference you'll taste with French AOC butters—they have a minimum of 84 percent butterfat, but often weigh in at 86 percent. That said, every recipe in this book was successfully tested with Land O'Lakes Unsalted (a.k.a. sweet) Butter, with 80 percent butterfat. As good as these recipes are with *beurre ordinaire,* I would love for you to try them with a French or premium-grade American butter. If you can find a French AOC butter, by all means use it. If not, look for a commercial French butter, Land O'Lakes Ultra-Creamy Unsalted Butter (it has 83 percent butterfat), or, better yet, an artisanally made American butter; my favorite is Vermont Butter & Cheese Company Cultured Butter, with a whopping 86 percent butterfat, the same as France's finest.

Madeleines

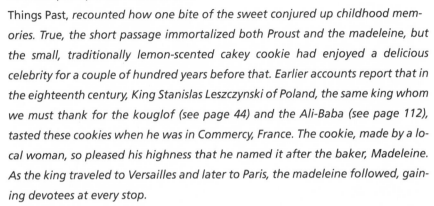

For generations, the shell-shaped madeleine has been tied to Marcel Proust, who, in Remembrance of Things Past, *recounted how one bite of the sweet conjured up childhood memories. True, the short passage immortalized both Proust and the madeleine, but the small, traditionally lemon-scented cakey cookie had enjoyed a delicious celebrity for a couple of hundred years before that. Earlier accounts report that in the eighteenth century, King Stanislas Leszczynski of Poland, the same king whom we must thank for the kouglof (see page 44) and the Ali-Baba (see page 112), tasted these cookies when he was in Commercy, France. The cookie, made by a local woman, so pleased his highness that he named it after the baker, Madeleine. As the king traveled to Versailles and later to Paris, the madeleine followed, gaining devotees at every stop.*

Because of the madeleine's light texture, its warm flavor, and its appealing shape, it is a favorite among pastry chefs, each of whom has a preferred recipe. Indeed, I probably could have collected enough madeleine recipes to fill this book—and I almost did. To give you just a hint of how versatile this madeleine is, I'm including three recipes: Classic Madeleines from André Lerch, whose eponymous pâtisserie faces La Tour d'Argent (see page 22); Honey Madeleines from Jean-Luc Poujauran, who works in the shadow of the Eiffel Tower (see page 34); and Earl Grey Madeleines from the famous tea company, Mariage Frères, at whose salons de thé these are a standard (see page 76).

A word on madeleine molds: *From the start, madeleines have been made in scallop-shaped molds, perhaps to commemorate the scallop shells worn by religious seekers on pilgrimages, perhaps not. These days, you can choose to make the fluted cookies large or small in traditional, nonstick, or even flexible silicone pans. If you are going out to buy pans, opt for nonstick. I can almost guarantee that if you have nonstick pans, you'll make madeleines twice as often. As for the silicone pans—they are nothing short of miraculous when it comes to nonstickability. However, they do give the fluted sides of the madeleines a slightly slick, somewhat shiny New Age look. You'll have to decide for yourself how much old-fashionedness you're willing to give up for remarkable convenience.*

Classic Madeleines / Madeleines Classiques

Adapted from Pâtisserie Lerch

¾ cup (105 grams) all-purpose flour

½ teaspoon double-acting baking
powder

2 large eggs, at room temperature

½ cup (100 grams) sugar

Grated zest of 1 lemon

2 teaspoons pure vanilla extract

5 tablespoons (2½ ounces; 70 grams)
unsalted butter, melted and
cooled

1. Sift together the flour and baking powder and keep close at hand. Working in a mixer fitted with the whisk attachment, beat the eggs and sugar together on medium-high speed until they thicken and lighten in color, 2 to 4 minutes. Beat in the lemon zest and vanilla. Switch to a large rubber spatula and gently fold in the dry ingredients, followed by the melted butter. Cover the batter with plastic wrap, pressing the wrap against the surface to create an airtight seal, and chill for at least 3 hours, preferably longer—chilling helps the batter develop its characteristic crown, known as the hump or bump. *(The batter can be kept tightly covered in the refrigerator for up to 2 days.)*

2. Center a rack in the oven and preheat the oven to 400°F (200°C). If your madeleine pan is *not* nonstick, generously butter it, dust the insides with flour, and tap out the excess. If the pan is nonstick, you still might want to give it an insurance coating of butter and flour. If it is silicone, do nothing. No matter what kind of pan you have, place it on a baking sheet for easy transportability.

3. Divide the batter among the molds, filling them almost to the top. Don't worry about smoothing the batter, it will even out as it bakes.

4. Bake large madeleines for 11 to 13 minutes, small ones for 8 to 10 minutes, or until the cookies are puffed and golden and spring back when touched. Pull the pan from the oven and remove the cookies by either rapping the pan against the counter (the madeleines should drop out) or gently running a butter knife around the edges of the cookies. Allow the madeleines to cool on a cooling rack. They can be served ever so slightly warm or at room temperature.

Honey Madeleines / Madeleines au Miel

Adapted from Boulangerie-Pâtisserie Poujauran

Reduce the sugar to ⅓ cup (65 grams) and use the zest from ½ lemon. Add 1 tablespoon honey along with the lemon zest and vanilla extract.

Earl Grey Madeleines / Madeleines au Thé Earl Grey

Adapted from Mariage Frères

Reduce the sugar to ⅓ cup (65 grams) and beat 2 tablespoons honey into the whipped eggs and sugar. Melt the butter, add 2 tablespoons Earl Grey tea (preferably Earl Grey Impériale from Mariage Frères; see the Source Guide, page 185), and allow the tea to infuse for 3 minutes before straining out the leaves and discarding them. Fold the butter into the batter at the end.

KEEPING: Stale madeleines, as Proust would be the first to tell you, are wonderful for dunking into hot tea. However, madeleine mavens who are not looking for dunkable sweets agree that madeleines are at their peak when they are freshly baked, just warm or at room temperature. The same fans, and I'm one of them, agree that if madeleines must wait, they should never wait more than a day. As soon as the madeleines-in-waiting are cool, pack them into an airtight container.

AN AMERICAN IN PARIS: Tampering with a classic is brazen, but the fact that so many French pastry chefs have done so gives me courage (as well as license). The easy tinker is to substitute orange zest for the lemon in the classic, but if you're feeling daring, you can add a couple teaspoons of orange-flower water along with the vanilla. Alternatively, you can drizzle the tiniest bit of orange-flower water over the madeleines as soon as you unmold them. It's also fun to toss a little spice into the classic batter. Try adding ¼ teaspoon ground cinnamon, ⅛ teaspoon freshly grated nutmeg, or even a pinch of ground coriander to the flour-and-baking-powder mix. And, if you're making M. Poujauran's honey madeleines, try using a big-flavored honey. I like either lavender or chestnut honey.

PÂTISSERIE LERCH

*P*âtisserie Lerch is a rustic pastry shop on a ritzy street. It is tucked into the small stretch of rue du Cardinal Lemoine that runs from the Seine to the boulevard Saint-Germain and counts as its neighbors the Île Saint-Louis, just across the river, and the legendary Tour d'Argent, just across the street. But over the quarter of a century or so that André Lerch has been on this street, he has worked more as though he were in a province of his native Alsace than in the center of one of the world's most exciting cities. His small shop, with its faded awning and old-fashioned double doors, is as homey as any country bakery, its sole decoration a trim of wreathed flowers, the symbol of Alsace.

It is Mme. Lerch who tends the front of the shop, presiding over small showcases filled with tarts and sugar buns and topped with enough cookies to keep a cache of school kids in smiles for days, and it is M. Lerche and his three helpers who bake the Classic Madeleines (page 20), spiced tea cakes, Anise Cookies (page 26), twisty kouglofs, and savory onion tarts that make his shop a daily stop for Parisians craving the specialties of northeastern France, the touchstones of his repertoire.

A pastry chef for more than forty years, André Lerch is at his shop before dawn, and several times a week he goes to the market to choose his own fruits, many of which he ripens himself so that he can be certain they will be perfect for his tarts. At midday, he and his wife have lunch together, and in the afternoon, the small oilcloth-covered table that is just on the other side of the kitchen is laid with a teatime snack that is often shared with friends who drop in, the way neighbors might in a small village.

Indeed, one day I visited M. Lerch late in the day, and I wasn't the only one who'd come by for cookies and conversation. The schoolchildren had already bought their treats and M. Lerch had already had his little *sieste*, the short nap he takes after lunch, when we met to taste a handful of his *pain d'épices*. Translated as "spice bread," and often referred to as gingerbread or, depending on the recipe, *lebkuchen, pain d'épices* can be a loaf cake, a soft cookie, or a very crunchy biscuit. In one version, a version M. Lerch is known for, the dough is left to ripen in a cool place for six months—hardly the recipe for an impatient baker or an impetuous snacker.

That afternoon, as we compared one delicious *pain d'épices* to another, we were joined by one of M. Lerch's army buddies. They'd known each other for fifty years and, although they no longer lived near each other nor saw each other often, they spoke as old friends do, easily and with the familiarity that allows for a kind of conversational shorthand. The friend pulled out pictures of the house he'd built in the South of France, and M. Lerch showed off a photo of a huge *pain d'épices* heart he'd made for his birthday party. As we were saying good-bye, M. Lerch winked and said, "My friend's the lucky one—he's a builder and his work lasts forever; I'm a baker and my work disappears almost as soon as I finish it." Looking at the pastry chef's devilish dimpled smile, how could I believe a word of it?

Lemon Butter Cookies / Sablés au Citron

Adapted from Pâtisserie Lerch

Cookies don't get simpler or more satisfying than sablés, *the basic butter cookie of France. They are homey, simple cookies that are sometimes flavored not at all (the better to show off their wholesome all-butter goodness) and sometimes given a spot of flavor, subtle or bold. At old-fashioned Pâtisserie Lerch (see page 22), M. Lerch, whose affection for cookies is evident (see also his Anise Cookies, page 26, and his Classic Madeleines, page 20), generously flavors his* sablés *with lemon zest and coats their edges with sugar so they emerge from the oven with a touch of sparkle. Because the dough is made with confectioners' sugar, the cookies are softer and more tender than most butter cookies, but because they are rolled into logs and sliced-and-baked, they are easier to make than many of their buttery brethren. There are just two things you must remember when you make these* sablés, *tips M. Lerch passed along to me. First, be gentle when you mix in the flour. Tender cookies depend on a tender touch, so you don't want to rough up the flour and activate the gluten. Second, give the logs of dough a nice long rest in the refrigerator. Refrigerating the dough relaxes the gluten and also helps the cookies hold their shape during slicing and baking.*

2 sticks (8 ounces; 230 grams) unsalted butter, at room temperature

⅔ cup (70 grams) confectioners' sugar, sifted

2 large egg yolks, at room temperature

Pinch of salt

2 teaspoons pure vanilla extract

Grated zest of 1 to 1½ lemons (to taste)

2 cups (280 grams) all-purpose flour

Approximately ½ cup (100 grams) sugar, for coating

1. Put the butter in the bowl of a mixer fitted with the paddle attachment and beat at medium speed until it is smooth. Add the sifted confectioners' sugar and beat again until the mixture is smooth and silky. Beat in 1 of the egg yolks, followed by the salt, vanilla, and grated lemon zest. Reduce the mixer speed to low and add the flour, beating just until it disappears. It is better to underbeat than overbeat at this point; if the flour isn't fully incorporated, that's OK—just blend in whatever remaining flour needs blending with a rubber spatula. Turn the dough out onto a counter, gather it into a ball, and divide it in half. Wrap each piece of dough in plastic wrap and refrigerate for about 30 minutes.

2. Working on a smooth surface, form each piece of dough into a log that is about 1 to 1¼ inches (2.5 to 3.2 cm) thick. (Get the thickness right, and the length you end up with will be fine.) Wrap the logs in plastic and chill for 2 hours. *(The dough can be wrapped airtight and kept refrigerated for up to 3 days or stored in the freezer for up to 1 month.)*

3. Position the racks to divide the oven into thirds and preheat the oven to 350°F (180°C). Line two baking sheets with parchment paper.

4. While the oven is preheating, work on the sugar coating: Whisk the remaining egg yolk in a small bowl until it is smooth and liquid enough to use as a glaze. Spread the sugar out on a piece of wax paper. Remove the logs of dough from the refrigerator, unwrap them, and brush them lightly with a little egg yolk. Roll the logs in the sugar, pressing the sugar gently to get it to stick if necessary, then, using a sharp slender knife, slice each log into cookies about ¼ inch (7 mm) thick. (You can make these thicker if you'd like; just bake them longer.) Place the cookies on the lined baking sheets, leaving about ½ inch (1.5 cm) space between them.

5. Bake the cookies for 12 to 14 minutes, or until they are set but not browned. (It's fine if the yolk-brushed edges brown a smidgen.) Transfer the cookies to cooling racks to cool to room temperature.

KEEPING: Packed airtight, the cookies will keep for about 5 days at room temperature. Because the sugar coating will melt, these cookies are not suitable for freezing.

AN AMERICAN IN PARIS: I've made these tender, sweet cookies at Christmas time and dolled them up by rolling them in larger-grained sugar. They're fun rolled in crystal sugar, which gives them a bit of crunch, and pretty rolled in dazzle sugar. You could even roll them in colored sugar to add dash to a tin of assorted cookies.

Anise Cookies / Pains d'Anis

Adapted from Pâtisserie Lerch

As plain as these cookies look, that's how surprising they are. At first glance, they have the look of little meringue buttons: their tops are pale, smooth, buff colored, and as crackly thin as parchment. Tucked beneath the crust is the cookie proper, a tidbit that is all crunch. These are cookies you might be tempted to gobble like gumdrops if it weren't for their flavor: anise, a flavor so assertive it can never be taken lightly. For those unfamiliar with anise, it has a bold licorice flavor and a full, almost floral fragrance, and both qualities are played up in these cookies, which are traditional in Switzerland and Alsace, pastry chef André Lerch's homeland, the root of his inspiration, and the source of so many of the most sought-after specialties in his shop (see page 22). If you love anise, I can guarantee you'll adore these. If anise is not your favorite flavor, see my vanilla variation, following the recipe.

A word on preparation: Although the batter is made in under 10 minutes, once piped or spooned out, the rounds need to rest for 24 hours—so plan ahead. In addition, unless you use a buttered and floured baking sheet, the cookies will not develop the craggy little circle at their base ("the foot"), which is characteristic of authentic pains d'anis.

2 cups (400 grams) sugar

3 tablespoons (15 grams) anise seeds

4 large eggs, at room temperature

2 cups (280 grams) all-purpose flour

1. **THE DAY BEFORE:** Butter two baking sheets, dust the sheets with flour, and shake off the excess. If you want to pipe the cookies, fit a medium pastry bag with a ⅜-inch (1-cm) plain round tip and set it aside; if not, you can use a small spoon.

2. Put the sugar and anise seeds in the work bowl of a food processor fitted with the metal blade and process for a full minute to flavor the sugar with the anise. Pour the sugar through a strainer into the bowl of a mixer; discard the anise seeds that remain in the strainer. Crack the eggs into the bowl, then, working with the whisk attachment, whip the eggs and sugar on high speed until they are thick and pale, about 3 minutes. When you lift the whisk, the mixture should fall back on itself and form a slowly dissolving ribbon. Switch to a large rubber spatula and, adding it through a strainer, gently fold in the flour in two additions.

3. Pipe or spoon rounds of the batter, each about 1¾ to 2 inches (about 5 cm) across, onto the baking sheets, leaving about ½ inch (1.5 cm) space between them. Allow the cookies to rest uncovered overnight at room temperature.

4. Position the racks to divide the oven into thirds and preheat the oven to 350°F (180°C).

5. Bake the cookies for 15 to 18 minutes, rotating the pans front to back and top to bottom midway, or until they have turned pale, almost white, on top and have formed a rough little foot at the base. Transfer the cookies to a rack and cool to room temperature.

KEEPING: Because these cookies are crisp and dry, they can be kept at room temperature in a covered container—or even an open basket—for at least a week.

AN AMERICAN IN PARIS: Instead of grinding anise seeds into the sugar, I sometimes grind in one or two vanilla bean pods—not the pristine pods that still have moist pulp, but the dried leftovers from other recipes (see page 29). If you haven't been stockpiling used pods, you can make these cookies by beating 4 teaspoons pure vanilla extract into the whipped egg mixture.

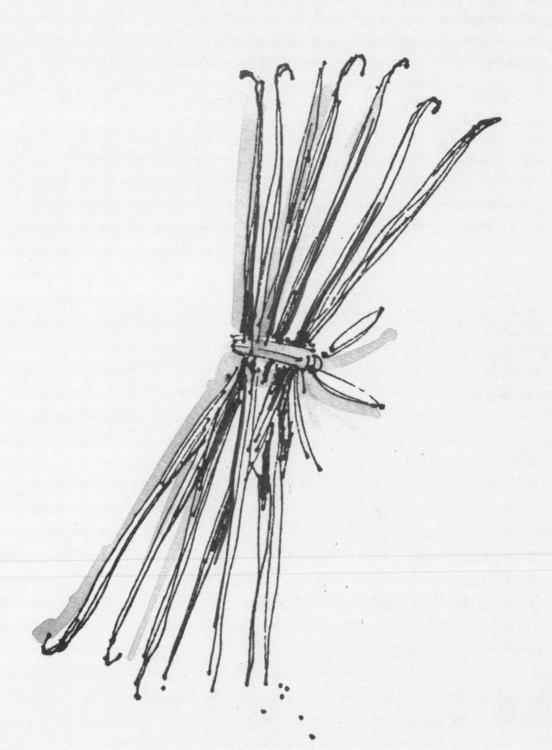

Vanilla

Vanilla is the culinary equivalent of the C-major chord in music, the backbone of so many great creations. It is the flavor that neutralizes the egginess of eggs, lays the groundwork on which other flavors can be built, and acts like the mother hen of a recipe, gathering all other flavors around it. Given its role in desserts, it is not surprising that Paris pastry chefs are very fussy about the kind of vanilla they use. For the most part, when there's vanilla in a recipe, it is in the form of a vanilla bean. (When chefs use extract, they use only pure vanilla extract—and you should do the same. Imitation vanilla extract, with its harsh, clearly fake flavor, will spoil whatever you put it into.) Vanilla beans are harvested from orchid plants, boiled, and then sun- or oven-dried until the pods, still plump, moist, and flexible (the signs, along with fragrance, of good beans), develop a frosting of shiny crystals. The most prized—and most expensive—beans are grown in Tahiti, Mexico, and Madagascar (where the beans are labeled "Bourbon"), and pastry chefs use every bit of them. If chefs are infusing milk or cream with the flavor of vanilla, they'll split the bean lengthwise, scrape out the aromatic pulpy seeds, and toss both pod and pulp into the pot. Then, when the job is done, they'll scoop out the pod, rinse it, and dry it in a warm oven or on the counter. Dried, the bean can be plunged into a canister of sugar or ground with sugar in a food processor; in either case, the result is great vanilla sugar. When you get good vanilla beans (beans that are plump, moist, fragrant, and perhaps even shiny and speckled with white crystals), treat them like the treasures they are: wrap them in a triple thickness of plastic film, then give them a final foil wrap, and keep them in the refrigerator. It's a lot of wrapping, but each time you undo the layers you'll be rewarded with a burst of vanilla fragrance, a treat worth the effort. In addition, all this protection means your beans will keep for months.

Orange Galettes / Galettes à l'Orange

Adapted from Maison Kayser

Just a couple of doors down from Eric Kayser's always-busy boulangerie on rue Monge (see page 116) is his pâtisserie, a shop whose décor is landmarked and whose front-room desserts are finished with flourishes. But just beyond that front room, above the counter with the sandwiches made on rustic organic bread, is a display of simple cookies, and stacked among them are Kayser's galettes à l'orange, a sweet I've come to think of as an orange-meringue tart masquerading as a cookie. It's a hybrid of sorts—sort of a cookie, sort of a tartlet, and every sort of snackable. Its base is a thin round of appropriately cookie-sweet tart dough, which you get just a glimpse of around the edges of the finished cookie. Taking up most of the real estate is a mix of Grand Marnier–spiked apricot jam topped with a swirling squiggle of crunchy meringue and a little piece of candied orange peel. It is a whimsical confection that teeters between a kid's treat and a grown-up's indulgence.

A word on the word galette: galette means many things in French. It was originally used to describe an ancient (perhaps the most ancient) cake, a patty of grains and cereals mashed down and baked on a sun-heated rock. Today the name is still used for flat cakes, as well as pancakes, sweet and savory; frequently used for open-faced tarts; very likely to turn up describing crêpes; and most likely to refer to a cookie, often a fat, flat, flaky Breton butter cookie.

THE COOKIE BASE

1¼ sticks (5 ounces; 140 grams) unsalted butter, at room temperature

½ cup (50 grams) confectioners' sugar

¼ cup (50 grams) sugar

¼ cup (25 grams) ground blanched almonds

Pinch of salt

1 large egg

1¾ cups (245 grams) all-purpose flour

1. **TO MAKE THE COOKIE BASE:** Working in a food processor or a mixer with the paddle attachment, beat the butter, confectioners' sugar, ground nuts, and salt together until the mixture is creamy but not airy. Mix in the egg and then the flour, mixing only until the flour is incorporated—no more. Turn out the dough, gather it into a ball, flatten it into a disk, and wrap it well in plastic. Chill it for at least 30 minutes. *(The dough can be wrapped airtight and kept refrigerated for up to 2 days or frozen for 1 month.)*

2. Line two baking sheets with parchment paper and keep them close at hand. Working on a lightly floured surface, roll the dough out to a thickness of about ¼ inch (7 mm). (The cookies need to be heftier than most because they will be supporting a fair amount of jam and meringue.) Using a large cookie cutter or

the rim of a 4-inch (10-cm) mini-tart pan, cut out as many rounds as you can. (If you like, you can gather the scraps together and reroll them.) Lift the rounds onto the baking sheets, prick them all over with the tines of a fork, and slip the sheets into the refrigerator to chill for about 20 minutes while you preheat the oven.

3. Position the racks to divide the oven into thirds and preheat the oven to 350°F (180°C).

4. Bake the cookies for 7 to 10 minutes, rotating the baking sheets top to bottom and front to back at the halfway point. The cookies will be pale and just firm. Transfer the sheets to cooling racks and let the cookies cool while you make the toppings.

5. **TO MAKE THE JAM AND MERINGUE:** Put the orange zest and apricot jam in the work bowl of a food processor or the jar of a blender and process until well combined. Add the Grand Marnier and pulse just to mix, then scrape the jam from the container and keep close at hand.

6. In a clean, dry mixer bowl, using the whisk attachment, beat the egg whites until they hold medium peaks. Still beating, add the sugar and continue to beat until the whites are firm but still glossy. Sift together the ground nuts and confectioners' sugar, and, using a rubber spatula, gently fold this into the beaten whites.

7. **TO ASSEMBLE THE GALETTES:** Using a butter knife or a small offset spatula, spread a thin layer of the jam over the cookies, leaving about ½ inch (1.5 cm) bare around the edges. Using a spoon or a pastry bag fitted with a small plain or star tip, cover the jam with meringue. Be generous with the meringue—it's nice to have a thick swirl on each cookie. Dust the cookies lightly with confectioners' sugar (use a sugar duster or sieve to sift the sugar onto the cookies) and put a bit of candied orange in the center of each cookie.

8. Bake for about 12 minutes, or until the cookies are firm and the meringue is set. Carefully lift the cookies onto a cooling rack using a wide metal spatula and cool to room temperature.

KEEPING: The cookies are best served the day they are made.

AN AMERICAN IN PARIS: I'm the only one in my little family with a passion for orange, so I sometimes split a batch of these, making a few orange cookies for myself and topping the remainder with raspberry jam spiked with a little framboise eau-de-vie.

THE JAM AND MERINGUE
Grated zest of 2 oranges
⅓ cup (120 grams) apricot jam
2 teaspoons Grand Marnier
2 large egg whites, preferably at
    room temperature
3 tablespoons (35 grams) sugar
⅓ cup (35 grams) ground toasted
    skinned hazelnuts or blanched
    almonds
⅓ cup (35 grams) confectioners'
    sugar

Confectioners' sugar for dusting
Small bits of candied orange peel for
    decorating the cookies (optional)

Simple Cakes

for

Snacks, Suppers, and "Le Goûter"

BOULANGERIE-
PÂTISSERIE
POUJAURAN

I can remember the first time I went to Jean-Luc Poujauran's bakery sometime in the 1980s. I was staying at the other end of Paris, but I made the pilgrimage happily because I'd heard so much about this young baker. What I hadn't heard about, and what made me smile with a girlish ear-to-ear grin, was how completely winning the little shop is. Tiny and painted in Provençal blue and cotton-candy pink, it is the kind of shop that makes even grown-ups want to press their noses up against the windowpanes—and many do.

No matter how many times you see Poujauran's place, you're bound to smile when you come upon the funny pink-tongued Dalmatian painted beneath the right-hand window, the one lettered in burnished gold with the word *Pâtisserie*. Come to the shop from the other direction, and you'll be greeted by the window that says *Boulangerie* and shows off, in addition to well-worn linen-lined baskets piled high with croissants and brioche, small breakfast pastries and nut-studded rolls, a miniature model of the already mini pastry shop: only the *camionnette*, the small delivery truck that is usually parked out front, is missing from the maquette. The truck, too, is picture-book cute, neatly painted down to the hubcaps in shades of blue, given a touch of pink, and topped with a woven-reed bread basket, which, as quaint as it may look, is really very practical—it carries the breads that are delivered each day from this little shop to dozens of Paris's best restaurants.

Actually, it was as a bread baker that Jean-Luc Poujauran, a native of France's southwestern region, made his name. But stand at the door and you'll notice that most people leave carrying a bread in one hand and a box of cookies or cakes in the other. His sweets, most of them quite simple, are irresistible. His pound cakes, or *quatre-quarts,* plain and chocolate (page 36), are the kind those of us whose grandmothers baked remember from childhood. His small almond *financiers* (page 16) and madeleines (page 20) are among the best in Paris, and he makes a wonderful version of a miniature cake from Bordeaux called *cannelé,* which is crusty and very dark on the outside and custardy on the inside.

It always takes more time than you think it will to make a choice chez Poujauran because the selection is wide, the details of the turn-of-the-last-century shop too cunning to ignore, and the way in which the breads and cakes, cookies, jams, and even wines are displayed so appealing that you are always distracted from the job of making a decision.

And speaking of distractions, did I mention the baker? I don't think I've ever read anything about Jean-Luc Poujauran that didn't mention his "movie-star" good looks—and with good reason: he is as adorable as he is talented, which is to say, he's very adorable. The shop, the sweets, and the baker are such a wonderful combination that I've often thought it might be the neighborhood's most treasured attraction, even though the Eiffel Tower is just down the street.

Chocolate Pound Cake I
Quatre-Quarts au Chocolat

Adapted from Boulangerie-Pâtisserie Poujauran

As quintessentially French as a quatre-quarts is, it's hard not to see it as the American pound cake's next of kin, a moist loaf cake with great keeping qualities, the kind of cake you like to have around for anytime nibbling. The name means "four quarters," and it refers to the classic four ingredients in this type of cake, as well as to the fact that the ingredients are used in equal proportions. Traditionally, a quatre-quarts is made by weighing 3 whole eggs—to get the mathematical base, so to speak—and then weighing out equivalent amounts of sugar, flour, and butter. The proportions for the quatre-quarts from bread baker/pastry chef Jean-Luc Poujauran (see page 34) are almost traditional, give or take a few grams here and there, but the use of brown sugar and the inspired addition of chocolate, while timelessly delicious, are not recorded in the history books—a grievous oversight.

4 ounces (115 grams) bittersweet chocolate, finely chopped

1¼ cups (175 grams) all-purpose flour

1 teaspoon double-acting baking powder

1¼ sticks (5 ounces; 140 grams) unsalted butter, at room temperature

1 cup (180 grams) packed light brown sugar

4 large eggs, at room temperature

1 large egg yolk, at room temperature

⅓ cup (85 grams) crème fraîche, homemade (page 50) or store-bought, or heavy cream

1. Center a rack in the oven and preheat the oven to 350°F (180°C). Butter four 5¾ x 3 x 2½-inch (14.5 x 7.5 x 6.5-cm) disposable aluminum foil mini loaf pans. Dust the insides of the pans with flour, tap out the excess, and put the pans on an insulated baking sheet or on two stacked regular baking sheets.

2. Melt the chocolate in a bowl over—not touching—simmering water or in a microwave oven; set it aside. Whisk the flour and baking powder together and set aside as well.

3. Working in a mixer fitted with the paddle attachment, beat the butter on medium speed until it is smooth and light. Add the sugar and beat for 2 minutes. One by one, add the whole eggs and the yolk, beating for 1 minute after each addition. Don't be concerned when the mixture curdles—it will come together when you add the dry ingredients. Reduce the mixer speed to low and beat in the cream, followed by the melted chocolate. When the chocolate is thoroughly incorporated, add the dry ingredients, mixing only until they disappear into the batter.

4. Divide the batter evenly among the pans. Bake the cakes for 35 to 40 minutes, or until a knife inserted into the center comes out clean. Transfer the cakes to a

cooling rack and cool for about 5 minutes before unmolding; turn the cakes right side up and cool to room temperature.

KEEPING: Wrapped airtight, the cakes will keep for 4 days at room temperature or for 1 month in the freezer.

AN AMERICAN IN PARIS: I sometimes spice up this cake by adding 1½ teaspoons ground cinnamon or ¼ teaspoon freshly grated nutmeg to the dry ingredients or by beating the grated zest of 1 orange into the batter when I'm beating the eggs and sugar together. In fact, if you like the flavor of orange with chocolate, you might want to fold about ½ cup chopped candied orange peel into the batter before you spoon it into the loaf pans.

Chocolate Almond Cake

Pain de Gênes au Chocolat

Adapted from Christian Constant

Leave it to the French to turn any occasion, even a bitter conflict, into the opportunity to create something delicious. Case in point, this homey almond cake, pain de Gênes, or "Genoa bread," which was invented to commemorate the 1800 siege of that Italian city. During the siege, people survived in large part on almonds, never, of course, concocted into anything this good, but the connection of Genoa and almonds was enough for an enterprising chef to create a cake that has remained a standard in the French repertory for generations.

The original and still most common version of this cake is flavored with rum or kirsch (see page 52) and includes not a drop of chocolate. But there is nothing common about this recipe, since it comes from one of Paris's least common chocolatiers, Christian Constant (see page 108), who has been making chocolate history in Paris for more than twenty years. Here, M. Constant takes the classic and turns it to his taste, adding cocoa and flavoring the cake with Cointreau, the orange-flavored liqueur, which combines to advantage with chocolate and almonds. A pain de Gênes *is usually served unglazed—and this* pain de Gênes *is just fine that way—but M. Constant suggests that if you want to give the cake extra zing, you finish it with a thin coating of orange marmalade. Just heat the marmalade until it liquefies and brush it over the cake, then let it set before serving.*

1. Center a rack in the oven and preheat the oven to 350°F (180°C). Butter an 8 x 2-inch (20 x 5-cm) round cake pan, line the bottom with parchment or wax paper, and butter the paper; dust the entire pan with flour and tap out the excess.

2. Sift together the potato starch and cocoa and set aside. Leave 1 of the eggs whole and separate the remaining 3 eggs.

3. Working in a mixer fitted with the paddle attachment, beat the ground almonds, confectioners' sugar, whole egg, and 3 egg yolks on medium speed for about 3 minutes, until the mixture is smooth and light. Beat in the Cointreau and vanilla, then reduce the mixer speed to low and add the sifted dry ingredients, mixing only until they are incorporated. If you don't have two bowls for your mixer, transfer the batter to a larger mixing bowl.

4. Working in a clean, dry mixer bowl, using the whisk attachment, beat the egg whites until they form soft peaks. Sprinkle in the granulated sugar and continue to beat until the whites are firm and glossy. With a rubber spatula, stir one-quarter of the whites into the batter, then gently fold in the rest of the whites. Very delicately, fold in the melted butter.

5. Scrape the batter into the pan, smooth the top, and slide the pan into the oven. Bake for 35 to 40 minutes, or until a knife inserted in the center of the cake comes out clean. Transfer to a rack to cool for 5 minutes before unmolding, then cool to room temperature right side up.

KEEPING: The cake can be wrapped airtight and kept at room temperature for 4 days or frozen for 1 month.

AN AMERICAN IN PARIS: If you think as I do that too much chocolate is never enough, try finishing this cake with a thin layer of chocolate glaze (page 148). If you'd like, replace the Cointreau with coffee-flavored Kahlúa or almond-flavored amaretto; even licorice-flavored Pernod or Ricard would be good here.

¼ cup (40 grams) potato starch (available in the baking or kosher foods section of most supermarkets)

¼ cup (25 grams) Dutch-processed cocoa powder

4 large eggs, at room temperature

1 cup (3½ ounces; 100 grams) finely ground blanched almonds

1 cup (100 grams) confectioners' sugar, sifted

2 teaspoons Cointreau or other orange-flavored liqueur

1 teaspoon pure vanilla extract

1 tablespoon (15 grams) sugar

1 stick (4 ounces; 115 grams) unsalted butter, melted and cooled

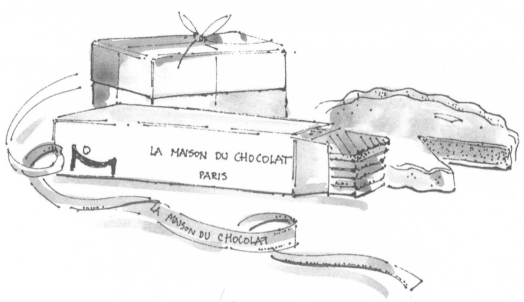

LA MAISON DU CHOCOLAT

La Maison du Chocolat is the perfect name for the house that master chocolatier Robert Linxe built. The exterior of every Maison du Chocolat is the color of the world's best bittersweet chocolate, a hue to put you in mind of lush truffles, impossibly creamy mousses, and cakes with chocolate glazes so glossy you can see your reflection in them. Inside, you are surrounded by milk-chocolate and caramel-colored walls and made light-headed by the potent perfume of chocolate. For those of us who believe that chocolate is, as its ancient name, *Theobrome,* decreed, the fruit of the gods, a step into La Maison du Chocolat is a step into chocolate heaven.

You don't have to know much about chocolate to know that a place like La Maison du Chocolat could only have been built by someone impassioned by the ingredient. And Robert Linxe is. One of eleven children, he was brought up in the Basque region of France. His father worked for the SNCF, the national railroad company, and raised his children in what M. Linxe (he is always referred to as Monsieur Linxe) has called "the cult of hard work." The children were expected to choose a vocation early and to commit themselves to it. For Robert Linxe, the choice was easy—he wanted to be a pastry chef. What wasn't easy was convincing his family that he had chosen wisely. "In the late 1940s," M. Linxe confided, "the job of pastry chef was not esteemed. In fact, if you didn't do well in school, the teachers recommended you become a pastry chef." Fortunately for chocolate connoisseurs around the world, Linxe *père* saw how serious his young son was and sent him off to study in Switzerland. His parting words to the aspiring chef were, "Remember, there's never a place for those who finish last."

The elder Linxe need not have worried—last was never a possibility for his son. From the time he opened his first shop in Paris in 1955 until the present, M. Linxe has set the standard for chocolate, making his name as a sorcerer of ganache, producing a ganache, the most luxurious filling for a chocolate bonbon, that is hyper-silken and perfectly balanced, and fashioning the shells for all his candies in sheets so thin even veteran chocolatiers marvel.

Now in his seventies, M. Linxe has ceded the daily operations of the Maison du Chocolat dynasty to Pascal Le Gac, who has worked with him for more than twenty years. What he has not ceded is his commitment to quality. M. Linxe still tastes every chocolate vintage (like wine, cocoa beans and the chocolate they are made into have vintages, which vary in quality because of weather and handling), still chooses each new line of desserts and chocolates, and still serves as an ambassador for French chocolates around the world, for La Maison du Chocolat's reputation extends around the world. From New York to Tokyo, people who adore chocolate know such Linxe classics as his Chocolate Mousse (page 106); the Bacchus (page 140), a heady rum-raisin chocolate cake; and the multitude of chocolates. Many of the chocolates, like the Traviata, a blend of chocolate and caramelized almonds, take their names from M. Linxe's love of music. People everywhere also know the caramel-colored La Maison du Chocolat box, the box that took six months to design and is made by the same box maker who fashions Hermès's signature packaging. The box may cost as much to produce as you'd pay for a slice of M. Linxe's irresistible Gâteau au Chocolat Grand-Mère (page 42), but it's M. Linxe's gift to you whenever you treat yourself to a handful of La Maison du Chocolat treasures.

Grandmother's Creamy Chocolate Cake / Gâteau au Chocolat Grand-Mère

Adapted from La Maison du Chocolat

I know for sure that Monsieur La Maison du Chocolat, Robert Linxe (see page 40), and I are not related—no one in my family is the least bit French—so we certainly could not have had grandmothers with anything in common. Yet as soon as I tasted his grandmother's cake, I thought of the cakes my own grandmother had made, the unfussed-over cakes that despite, or maybe even because of, their simplicity, hold a place in my affections all these years later.

Like the memorable cakes of my American childhood, M. Linxe's French grandmother's cake has a humble look and a haunting flavor. It is a thoroughly chocolate, stirred-in-a-saucepan treat with only five ingredients and a smooth, dense interior that is more like fudge than cake, and more delectable for being so.

2 sticks (8 ounces; 230 grams) unsalted butter, cut into 16 pieces

8 ounces (230 grams) bittersweet chocolate, finely chopped

¾ cup (150 grams) sugar

4 large eggs, at room temperature

¼ cup (35 grams) all-purpose flour

Whipped cream, crème fraîche (homemade, page 50, or store-bought), or vanilla ice cream for serving (optional)

1. Center a rack in the oven and preheat the oven to 300°F (150°C). Butter an 8-inch (20-cm) square pan and line it with aluminum foil. Have ready a larger pan that can hold the cake pan and water (to make a bain-marie).

2. Put the butter in a heavy medium saucepan, then add the chocolate and the sugar. Place the pan over medium-low heat and, stirring almost constantly, heat until the butter, chocolate, and sugar are melted and well blended. Remove the pan from the heat and set it on the counter for 3 minutes.

3. One by one, stir the eggs into the chocolate mixture, using a whisk. Sift the flour over the mixture and stir it in as well. Rap the saucepan on the counter to deflate any air bubbles and pour the batter into the prepared pan.

4. Put the cake pan into the larger pan, fill the larger pan with enough hot water to come halfway up the sides of the cake pan, and slip the setup into the oven. Bake for 35 to 40 minutes, or until the cake is set on top and a knife inserted in the center comes out streaky but not wet. Lift the cake pan out of the water bath and place it on a rack to cool to room temperature. Chill the cake for at least 1 hour before unmolding.

5. When the cake is cold, gently turn it over onto a serving platter, lift off the pan, and carefully remove the foil. The cake is meant to be served upside down, with

its sleeker side facing the world. If you'd like, it can be served cold or at room temperature with a scoop of whipped cream, crème fraîche, or ice cream.

KEEPING: The cake can be kept, tightly wrapped, in the refrigerator for 2 to 3 days. Wrapped airtight, it can be frozen for a month.

AN AMERICAN IN PARIS: I cut leftover cake into tiny cubes, freeze the cubes, and either churn them into homemade ice cream (add the chunks just a minute before the ice cream is ready to be removed from the machine) or stir them into softened best-quality store-bought ice cream. Because the cake's texture is so luxuriously soft, it will not harden completely in the freezer; rather, it will firm and become just a little chewy.

Kouglof

Adapted from Pâtisserie Stéphane Vandermeersch

Alsace is the birthplace of the kouglof, but all of France has taken this yeasty raisin-studded sweet to its heart. The base of the kouglof is what the French call "a poor brioche," that is, it is made with a brioche dough that has fewer eggs and less butter than the norm. In fact, this dough even substitutes water for the usual milk. The cake is kept "lean" and a little dry because it is finished with a soaking syrup, in this case one that is scented with orange-flower water. The orange-flower water is a lovely touch from pastry chef Stéphane Vandermeersch (see page 162), who has made a name for his small shop near the Bois de Vincennes by giving pride of place (and sometimes a little tweak) to the classics. The kouglof's traditional finish is a soak of melted butter or no soak at all— many kouglof admirers admire a dry cake. What remains un-changed in this rendition is the traditional shape of the cake: it is made in a tube pan, aptly called a kouglof pan, with a twisty, curvy Turk's head pattern. (If you don't have a 9-inch [24-cm] kouglof pan, you can use a 9-inch [24-cm] Bundt pan instead.)

In France, the kouglof is often served for break-fast—it is a time-honored Sunday indulgence— or at teatime, and it is considered by many to be at its prime only after it has been left on the counter for a day to stale a bit. I've always thought that the reason it is left to stale is so that it will soak up that much more café au lait when you dunk it.

A word on preparation: *Brioche dough is best made in a heavy-duty stand mixer, and even with a mixer, it will take a while for the dough to be-come smooth and satiny and for it to pull away from the sides of the bowl. If you're concerned that your mixer won't stand up to 15 minutes or so of hard labor, check the manufacturer's booklet. (My KitchenAid stand mixer has no problem with brioche.)*

1. **TO MAKE THE CAKE**: Put the yeast and water in the bowl of a heavy-duty mixer and stir with a wooden spoon until the yeast is dissolved. Add the flour and salt and stir to just moisten the flour; you'll have a shaggy, fairly dry mass. Fit the bowl into the mixer and attach the dough hook. Put the eggs and yolk in a small bowl and beat them lightly with a fork.

2. Mixing on low speed, add the eggs to the yeast mixture, beating until they are incorporated. Add the sugar, increase the mixer speed to medium-high, and beat, scraping down the bowl as needed, until the dough smooths out a bit and comes together, about 5 minutes. Lower the speed to medium and add the butter one piece at a time, squeezing each piece in your hand to soften it before you add it. When the butter is fully incorporated, the dough will be very soft. Increase the mixer speed to medium-high and continue to beat, scraping down the bowl now and then, until the dough is smooth and satiny, pulls away from the sides of the bowl, and climbs up the hook, about 8 to 10 minutes. Remove the bowl from the mixer.

3. Bring a small amount of water to the boil in a saucepan, drop in the raisins, turn off the heat, and allow the raisins to steep for a minute. Drain the raisins, pat them dry between paper towels, and mix them into the dough with a wooden spoon.

4. Transfer the dough to a clean bowl, cover with plastic wrap, and leave at room temperature until the dough nearly doubles in size, about 45 minutes.

5. Deflate the dough by lifting it up around the edges and letting it fall back with a slap. Cover the bowl with plastic wrap and put it in the refrigerator, "slapping" down the dough every 30 minutes until it stops rising, about 2 hours. (*At this point, the dough can be wrapped tightly in plastic wrap and kept refrigerated for up to 2 days.*)

6. Generously butter a 9-inch (24-cm) kouglof mold (see headnote). Remove the dough from the refrigerator and turn it onto a very lightly floured work surface. Work the dough into a smooth ball and flatten the ball slightly, then dust your fingers with flour. Use your thumb to work a hole in the center of the dough, then pull the dough gently to make the hole just large enough to fit over the center tube of the pan. Fit the dough into the pan, cover lightly with buttered parchment or wax paper, and allow the dough to rise for 1½ to 2 hours, or until it comes almost to the top of the pan.

7. While the dough is rising, center a rack in the oven and preheat the oven to 375°F (190°C).

THE CAKE

½ cube compressed yeast (0.3 ounces; 8 grams), crumbled, or ½ packet active dry yeast (scant ½ tablespoon; 3.5 grams)

⅓ cup (75 grams) water, at warm room temperature

2 cups (270 grams) all-purpose flour

2 pinches salt

2 large eggs, at room temperature

1 large egg yolk, at room temperature

2 tablespoons (25 grams) sugar

1 stick (4 ounces; 115 grams) butter, cut into 4 chunks, at room temperature

½ cup (80 grams) moist, plump raisins

8. Remove the paper and bake the kouglof for 10 minutes, then cover it lightly with a foil tent. Continue to bake for another 20 minutes, or until the kouglof is golden brown and has risen to the top or over the top of the pan. While the kouglof is baking, make the syrup.

9. **TO MAKE THE SYRUP:** Bring the sugar and water to the boil in a small saucepan, stirring to dissolve the sugar. Off the heat, whisk in the ground almonds and orange-flower water. Transfer the syrup to a bowl and set aside at room temperature until needed.

10. **TO FINISH THE CAKE:** As soon as the cake comes from the oven, unmold it onto a cooling rack placed over a rimmed baking sheet lined with foil. Using a pastry brush or a spoon, soak the cake evenly with the syrup. The cake is ready to serve as soon as it reaches room temperature.

KEEPING: Once the cake is soaked, it can be served immediately or wrapped in plastic wrap and kept at room temperature for a day or two.

AN AMERICAN IN PARIS: I like to cut thick slices of stale kouglof, toast them, and slather them with butter. They make a great breakfast treat. They're even a greater treat when you cover the butter with some good orange or lemon marmalade.

Le Goûter

Le goûter is to the French what afternoon tea is to the British: a little something, often sweet, to tide one over between lunch and dinner. And, like British tea, *le goûter* might once have been an actual meal served in the early evening when workers were coming in from the fields. Of course, there are no fields to come in from in Paris, unless you consider the playing fields in the Bois de Boulogne or the sunbathing terraces in front of Les Invalides, but the custom of nibbling after work or school has persisted and, in Paris, been deliciously citified. Between 4 and 6 P.M., after lunch and before it is time for an *apéritif,* cafés and *salons de thé* serve tartlets and cakes, ice cream sundaes, and cups of thick, steaming hot chocolate to capacity crowds. I've always loved this time in Paris. There's a coziness to being in a café surrounded by hot-chocolate sippers, a sense of ease and of indulgence. It's a lovely custom and a habit that's easy to slip into. Treat yourself to a *goûter* a couple of days in a row, and you'll find your tummy rumbling for a *tarte Tatin* around five in the afternoon. As long as there's a Parisian café in sight or a petite something in the cupboard (think madeleines [page 20], chocolate *quatre-quarts* [page 36], *pavé de Montmartre* [page 52], or, of course, a slice of *tarte Tatin* [page 78]), you've got nothing to do but give in and enjoy.

Lemon or Orange Cake /

Cake Citron ou Cake Orange

Adapted from Pâtisserie Arnaud Larher

You can use this recipe to make either a lemon or an orange cake. Whichever you choose, you'll get a beautifully tight-grained loaf cake with an intense citrus flavor. In the States, we think of cakes like these as pound cakes, but in France, they are called "weekend cakes" because they are sturdy (sturdy enough to be packed in a weekend picnic basket), keep well (they'll last the weekend and then some), and easy to enjoy with anything from Saturday morning coffee to Sunday afternoon tea. Not surprisingly, at Montmartre favorite Pâtisserie Arnaud Larher (see page 10), these weekend cakes sell out on weekdays too.

To get the most flavor out of the grated zest in this recipe, you mix the zest and sugar together with your fingertips, rubbing the two ingredients together until the sugar is moist and grainy and the piquant aroma of citrus fills the kitchen. Do this once, and you'll find yourself doing it often in other recipes.

2¼ cups (250 grams) cake flour, sifted

¾ teaspoon double-acting baking powder

¼ teaspoon salt

1⅔ cups (335 grams) sugar

Grated zest of 3 lemons or 2 oranges

5 large eggs, at room temperature

⅔ cup (165 grams) crème fraîche, homemade (page 50) or store-bought, or heavy cream, at room temperature

2 tablespoons (30 grams) dark rum (for the lemon cake) or Grand Marnier (for the orange cake)

7½ tablespoons (3¾ ounces; 110 grams) unsalted butter, melted and cooled

1. Center a rack in the oven and preheat the oven to 350°F (180°C). Butter and flour a 9 x 5 x 3-inch (22.5 x 12.5 x 7.5-cm) loaf pan, dust the interior with flour, and tap out the excess. Put the pan on an insulated baking sheet or on two stacked regular baking sheets and set aside.

2. Sift the flour, baking powder, and salt together and keep close at hand. Toss the sugar and zest together in a large bowl and rub them together with your fingertips until the sugar is moist and aromatic. Whisk in the eggs, beating until the mixture is pale and foamy, then whisk in the crème fraîche and rum. Switch to a large rubber spatula and gently stir the sifted flour mixture into the batter in three or four additions—the batter should be thick and smooth. Finally, fold in the cooled melted butter in two or three additions.

3. Immediately spoon the batter into the pan and slide the baking sheet(s) into the oven. Bake for 1 hour and 25 to 30 minutes, or until a thin knife inserted into the center of the cake comes out dry and free of crumbs. (Check the cake at the 40-minute mark. If it is browning quickly, cover it loosely with a foil tent for the remainder of the baking period.) Remove the cake from the oven and

allow it to cool for about 10 minutes on a cooling rack before turning it out of the pan; invert and cool to room temperature right side up.

KEEPING: Wrapped airtight, the cake will keep for 1 week at room temperature or up to 1 month in the freezer. Stale cake is delicious lightly toasted and spread with marmalade.

AN AMERICAN IN PARIS: I've used this recipe to make a wonderful vanilla cake. I substitute the pulp of 2 plump, fragrant vanilla beans for the zest and rub the pulp into the sugar just as the zest is rubbed in. Keep the rum in the recipe—it's lovely with the vanilla.

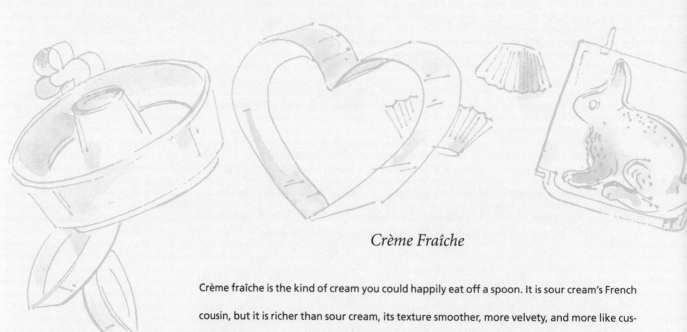

Crème Fraîche

Crème fraîche is the kind of cream you could happily eat off a spoon. It is sour cream's French cousin, but it is richer than sour cream, its texture smoother, more velvety, and more like custard. When you buy crème fraîche at an outdoor market or from a neighborhood cheese shop in Paris, it is spooned from a crock into a small container and, in the process, falls languidly off the ladle. In terms of taste, crème fraîche is tangy the way sour cream is tangy, but its tang is more subtle, more refined. And, unlike sour cream, crème fraîche can be whipped into soft peaks and cooked without risk of curdling. It is one of milk's minor miracles and is treated as such in Paris, where it is used often in a cake or tart recipe, piped into a rosette to top a mousse, spooned into a quenelle to finish a savory soup or a portion of sweet gâteau, dolloped on top of a sundae, and, yes, eaten off a spoon in the privacy of one's own kitchen when no one is looking.

The French take their crème fraîche seriously and Parisians will have a favorite merchant at the market from whom they'll buy their week's supply, or they'll look for *crème d'Isigny,* the one crème fraîche to be awarded AOC, or *Appellation d'Origine Contrôlée,* status. (This crème fraîche is made from the same cream as AOC butter from Isigny.) While any recipe that calls for crème fraîche can be made with regular heavy cream (*crème fleurette,* in

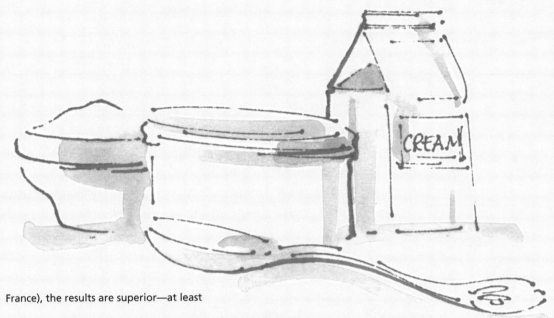

France), the results are superior—at least

in the sensuousness department—when the *crème* is thick, slightly acidic crème fraîche.

I remember the first time I made Gérard Mulot's Cherry Clafoutis (page 82) in Paris. Before the filling of crème fraîche, eggs with yolks the color of tangerines, and the pulp of deeply fragrant vanilla beans was poured into the crust to bake, I was ready to pour it into a glass and drink it like a shake. I recall turning to my husband and saying, "With ingredients this good, you really don't have to do much to make something spectacular."

Unfortunately, crème fraîche is not easily found in the United States and what is available is often very expensive. However, crème fraîche can be made simply and reasonably at home. To make 1 cup of crème fraîche, pour 1 cup heavy cream into a clean jar, add 1 tablespoon buttermilk or yogurt, cover the jar tightly, and shake it for about a minute. Then just leave the jar on the counter for 12 to 24 hours, or until the crème fraîche thickens slightly. How quickly it thickens will depend on the temperature of the room—the warmer the room, the quicker the thickening action. When it has thickened, chill the crème fraîche in the refrigerator for a day before you use it. Crème fraîche can be kept covered in the refrigerator for about 2 weeks and (or but, depending on your taste) will get tangier and tangier day after day.

Montmartre Square / Pavé Montmartre

Adapted from Pâtisserie Arnaud Larher

This cake epitomizes the appeal of the simple. Named for the colorful neighbor-hood lucky enough to claim Pâtisserie Arnaud Larher (see page 10) as its own, it is a moist almond cake, really a classic pain de Gênes (see page 38 for the history of this sweet) baked in a square pan so that it lives up to the pavé, or paving stone, part of its name. A mixture of nothing more than almond paste, eggs, but-ter, a splash of Grand Marnier or Kirsch , and a bit of flour to hold everything to-

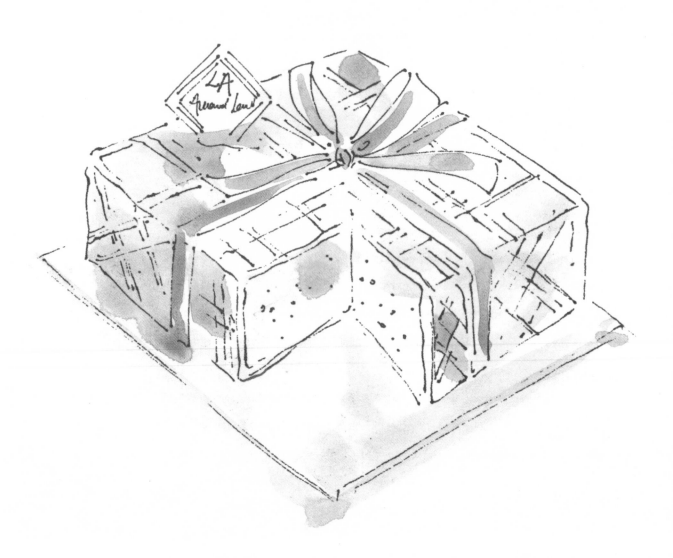

gether (it is like an old-fashioned one-bowl cake), the pavé is beaten for a full fif-teen minutes so that its texture is tender, its crumb fine, its light crust supple, and its keepability long.

At the shop, the cake is wrapped in an almond-paste cloak, which is glazed with egg and burnished to a golden brown in a hot oven. Arnaud Larher even ties the cake with ribbon. But as pretty as the almond coating is, it is entirely optional. Indeed, the French have been enjoying this cake sans décoration for generations. (See "An American in Paris" at the end of the recipe for an abbreviated version of this covering.)

A word on ingredients and gear: Your almond paste must be soft and your mixer must be strong. I wouldn't attempt this without a heavy-duty stand mixer. While you can make the cake in any kind of 8-inch (20-cm) square pan you have, for the most pavé-like pavé, it's best to have a pan with truly straight sides and squared-off corners. At the pastry shop, these cakes are available in various sizes. If you can find a 4-inch (10-cm) pan, buy two—you'll be able to make two cakes from this recipe, and they will be what I think of as the most adorable size for this sweet.

1. **TO MAKE THE CAKE**: Center a rack in the oven and preheat the oven to 350°F (180°C). Butter an 8-inch (20-cm) square pan (or two 4-inch/10-cm pans), dust the inside(s) with flour, tap out the excess, and put the pan(s) on a baking sheet.

2. Sift the flour and potato starch together and keep close at hand. Put the almond paste and 2 of the eggs in the bowl of a mixer fitted with the paddle attachment and beat on medium speed for 5 minutes. Scrape down the sides of the bowl, remove the paddle, and put the whisk attachment in place. Return the mixer to medium speed and beat in the remaining 2 eggs one at a time. Once the eggs are incorporated, beat the batter for another 10 minutes, scraping down the bowl frequently, until the almond paste is very creamy; it will remind you of mayonnaise.

3. Stir a couple of tablespoons of this batter into the cooled melted butter. Reduce the mixer speed to low and beat in the Grand Marnier followed by the dry in-gredients, mixing only until they are incorporated. Switch to a rubber spatula and gently fold in the butter.

THE CAKE

¼ cup (35 grams) all-purpose flour

2½ tablespoons (25 grams) potato starch (available in the baking or kosher foods section of most supermarkets)

14 ounces (2 tubes Odense brand; 400 grams) soft, pliable almond paste, broken into pieces

4 large eggs

1 stick (4 ounces; 115 grams) un-salted butter, melted and cooled

1 tablespoon Grand Marnier or kirsch

THE COVERING (OPTIONAL)
14 ounces (2 tubes Odense brand;
    400 grams) soft, pliable almond
    paste
2 large egg yolks, lightly beaten with
    1 tablespoon cold water

4. Turn the batter into the prepared pan(s) and bake for 35 to 40 minutes (the small pans will take about 35 minutes), or until the cake starts to pull away from the sides of the pan(s) and a knife inserted in the center comes out clean. Pull the cake(s) from the oven, unmold onto a cooling rack, and cool to room temperature upside down.

5. **TO COVER THE CAKE (OPTIONAL):** Press the two cylinders of almond paste together and mold them into a square. Working on a lightly floured work surface, roll out the almond paste until you have a square that is about 20 inches (50 cm) on a side. As you are rolling, make sure to lift the almond paste so that it doesn't stick to the counter, and turn it over so that you roll on both sides. Don't worry if your square is ragged; almond paste is as patchable as Play-Doh. Using a pastry brush, lightly coat the entire surface of the almond paste with beaten yolk. Place the cake upside down in the center of the square, then gently lift the almond paste up and around the cake, wrapping it like a present. To avoid bulges of almond paste in the corners, cut a "V" of almond paste from each corner. If needed, use the cutouts from the corners and any almond paste you've trimmed to fill in any bare spots.

6. Turn the cake right side up onto a parchment-lined baking sheet and brush the top and sides with a light coating of the beaten yolks. Wait for 5 minutes, then paint the top and sides of the cake again. Immediately, using the tines of a fork, etch a design—cross-hatching is nice—in the top and sides of the cake. Allow the cake to dry, open to the air, for at least 12 hours, preferably 24.

7. The next day, position a rack in the upper third of the oven and preheat the oven to 450°F (230°C).

8. Slide the cake, still on the parchment-lined baking sheet, into the oven and bake until the egg-yolk glaze turns golden, about 5 minutes. Check often, and pull the cake from the oven as soon as the color is right. It is ready to serve when the covering is cool.

KEEPING: A *pavé* without an almond-paste cloak will keep, well wrapped, for 5 days at room temperature or 1 month in the freezer. Cloaked, the cake will keep for a week at room temperature, but it should not be frozen.

AN AMERICAN IN PARIS: This cake has become a staple *chez moi*—I make one often, although rarely with its full almond-paste mantle. Usually I serve the cake plain and unadorned, but if I want to dress the cake up a smidge, I give it just a top coat of almond paste. Using one tube of almond paste, I roll out a square just large enough to cover the top of the cake, then proceed with the egg wash, decoration, and drying. To burnish it, I use a mini baker's blowtorch (available at Williams-Sonoma); alternatively, you can wrap the cake in foil, leaving the topping exposed, and hit the top with heat from the broiler.

**PIERRE HERMÉ
PARIS**

$\mathscr{P}$ierre Hermé always does the unexpected. In fact, perhaps the only thing he has ever done that was completely predictable was to become a pastry chef—and he was the fourth generation of Hermés to do that. "I don't think I had a choice," he says; "it was in my DNA." That he became one of France's best-known and most-respected pastry chefs just might have been in his DNA too.

Because I've known Pierre for more than a decade and collaborated with him on two cookbooks, I've had the fun of watching him work—and tasting his work—at many stages of his career. I didn't know Pierre when he was four-teen and the legendary Gaston Lenôtre (see page 72) asked his father if he could apprentice his young son. Nor did I know him when, at nineteen, he became the pastry chef at Lenôtre's flagship store. When we met, Pierre was the pastry chef at Fauchon (see page 128) and had just caused a sensation with his Cherry on the Cake, an extravagant, whimsical, delicious milk chocolate creation that was so singular it was written about in everything from *Le Monde* to an Italian architecture journal.

I remember walking through Fauchon's kitchens with Pierre and tasting as we went along. What was most memorable—and what I later came to realize was Pierre's hallmark—was that each time I tasted something I thought I knew well, it tasted slightly different from the classic, and that slight difference made it even better.

When Pierre became top toque at Ladurée (see page 96) and opened their spectacular shop on the Champs-Élysées, I saw him continue to create new recipes and revise older ones. Then, in 2000, Pierre created desserts for Korova, a Paris restaurant that became the must-go place for the city's hip, cool, and artistic crowd. With each new venture, his work became bolder and better until, as all the critics agree, it reached its peak (or at least its up-until-now peak) with the opening of his own shops.

These days, there is one place in the works, Pierre Hermé Rendez-vous, a breakfast-lunch-teatime restaurant and shop of temptations off the Champs-Elysées in the eighth *arrondissement,* and one in full swing, the bittersweet chocolate–colored jewel box in the Sixth, steps from Place Saint-Sulpice, forty-five seconds from Place Saint-Germain-des-Prés, and, what luck for me, one minute from my apartment. Now the hit parade of Pierre's signature sweets, among them the Cherry on the Cake; a collection of classics, including his Parisian Flan (page 58); a line-up of new desserts, including his elegant Coffee Tart (page 88); his outstanding breakfast pastries; all of his chocolates; and his seven cookbooks, two in English, five in French, have found a home.

Shortly after Pierre opened in the Sixth, I walked from the shop to Place Saint-Sulpice and found two chic American women nibbling greedily and giddily on the sweets they'd just bought. When I asked them the obvious, "Are you enjoying the pastries?" they answered with the obvious, a resounding "Yes!" and added, "We're eating as much as we can now, because we can't get this at home." Lots of us are waiting for a Pierre Hermé boutique in America. And there will be one—the question is when. Until there's a Pierre Hermé down the street from my New York apartment, in between my Paris sojourns, I'll keep making his creamy flan and batches of his chocolate–chocolate chip Korova Cookies (page 6). And you just might want to do that too.

Parisian Flan / Flan Parisien

Adapted from Pierre Hermé Paris

Most of us, when we hear the word flan, *think of a jiggly custard, maybe an upside-down crème caramel or perhaps a creamy tart speckled with a little fruit. But the flan that internationally celebrated pastry chef Pierre Hermé (see page 56) gives us is a tall, custardy cake contained in a pastry crust that is flakier than a typical French tart shell and more supple and fun to work with than most crusts, French or American. The filling, the flan part, is an unusual recipe—custardy, yes, but not at all rich. It is made just as we would make an old-fashioned American cornstarch pudding, but it is made from almost equal parts milk (not cream) and water, and it's the water that gives the flan its surprising lightness. Actually, for reasons not immediately apparent, giving the flan the recommended overnight chill also adds immeasurably to the unusually light and wholly satisfying texture of the filling.*

When Pierre gave me this recipe, he was quick to add that it is a truly Parisian recipe, documented as such in the Île-de-France (the French département that includes Paris) volume of The Inventory of France's Culinary Patrimony, *a well-researched book detailing the region's natural products and traditional recipes. He also said that he wanted me to have this recipe because it is one of his favorites and—now we're getting to the important part—it is completely delicious.*

1. **TO MAKE THE CRUST**: Put all of the ingredients except the flour in the bowl of a food processor and process until the mixture is soft and creamy. Add the flour and pulse in quick spurts until the dough forms a ball—then stop. Turn the dough out onto a smooth work surface, gather it together in a ball, and flatten it into a disk. Wrap the disk well in plastic wrap. Chill the dough for at least 4 hours. *(The dough can be kept in the refrigerator for up to 3 days or frozen for up to 1 month.)*

2. Line a baking sheet with parchment or wax paper and keep it close at hand. Working on a generously floured work surface, roll the dough out to a thickness of between ⅛ and ¼ inch (4 and 7 mm). Cut out a 12-inch (30-cm) circle of dough and transfer it to the lined baking sheet. Cover and chill the dough for at least 30 minutes.

3. Butter a 9-inch (24-cm) springform pan and put it on a parchment-lined baking sheet. (If you've got a 9-inch/24-cm cake ring that is 1¼ inches/3 cm high, it would be perfect for this flan.) Fit the dough into the pan, pressing it evenly along the bottom of the pan and up the sides. Trim the dough so that it comes 1¼ inches (3 cm) up the sides of the pan (if you're using a cake ring, just trim the dough even with the sides of the ring). Chill the dough for at least 2 hours and up to overnight.

4. Center a rack in the oven and preheat the oven to 350°F (180°C).

5. Line the crust with parchment paper and fill it with beans or rice. Bake the crust for 18 to 20 minutes, until it is set but not browned. Pull it from the oven, remove the paper and beans, and cool to room temperature.

6. **TO MAKE THE FILLING**: Bring the milk and water to the boil in a medium saucepan. Meanwhile, in another medium saucepan, preferably one with a heavy bottom, whisk the eggs, sugar, and cornstarch together.

7. Whisking without stop, drizzle one-quarter of the hot liquid over the egg mixture. When the eggs are warmed, add the rest of the liquid in a steady stream. Put the saucepan over medium heat and, whisking constantly and energetically, heat the filling just until it thickens and a couple of bubbles pop on the surface. Immediately pull the pan from the heat and push the filling through a sieve into a bowl. Let the filling cool on the counter for about 30 minutes.

8. **TO FINISH**: Center a rack in the oven and preheat the oven to 375°F (190°C).

9. Put the pan with the crust on a parchment-lined baking sheet (if it isn't still on one) and scrape the filling into the crust; smooth the top. Slide the baking sheet into the oven and bake the flan for 1 hour, or until the filling is puffed and just jiggles in the center when you tap the pan. Transfer the baking sheet to a cool-

THE CRUST

1 stick plus 5 tablespoons (6½ ounces; 180 grams) unsalted butter, at room temperature

½ teaspoon salt

½ teaspoon sugar

½ large egg yolk (lightly beat 1 yolk, then spoon out half)

3½ tablespoons (50 grams) whole milk

2 cups (280 grams) all-purpose flour

THE FILLING

1½ cups (375 grams) whole milk

1⅔ cups (370 grams) water

4 large eggs, preferably at room temperature

1 cup (200 grams) sugar

½ cup (60 grams) cornstarch, sifted

ing rack and let the flan cool to room temperature, then chill the flan for at least 6 hours, preferably overnight.

10. Serve the flan cold, the temperature at which the filling will seem lighter and, as Pierre Hermé says, *bien meilleur,* much better.

KEEPING: The flan needs a good chill before serving. It can be kept in the refrigerator for about 2 days.

AN AMERICAN IN PARIS: I don't often do much to this cake—I like it just the way it is—but I have tossed some fresh cherries into the filling, playing on the idea of clafoutis (see page 82), and have also added slices of sautéed-in-butter-and-sugar apples (much like the ones in the Toast-Point Apple Tart, page 74), or armagnac-soaked prunes, and have found myself, and my fellow indulgers, quite happy.

Tarts

for

Teatime or Anytime

Chocolate Tart / Tarte au Chocolat

Adapted from La Maison du Chocolat

Robert Linxe, the founder of La Maison du Chocolat (see page 42), is known for countless chocolate indulgences, but when I asked him to choose recipes for me, the first thing he said was, "You must have my chocolate tart." In many ways, the chocolate tart is the simplest of M. Linxe's creations, but in its simplicity it spotlights what is wondrous about chocolate: its flavor, of course, but also its luxurious good looks, its dizzying aroma, and its texture, which in this tart is melt-on-your-tongue seductive.

1. Put the chocolate in a heatproof bowl and keep it close at hand. In a small bowl, beat 1 tablespoon of the heavy cream with the egg yolks just until the eggs are liquid. Check that the butter is soft but not oily. If necessary, either beat it with a rubber spatula to soften it or smear it against the counter under the heel of your hand.

2. Pour the remaining cream into a saucepan, toss in the split vanilla bean, and bring the cream to a full boil. Pull out the vanilla bean, then pour the hot cream over the chocolate. Wait for about 30 seconds, then, working with a whisk, gently blend the cream into the chocolate. Still whisking delicately, incorporate the yolks, followed by the butter. Pour the ganache into the crust (if you have a little left over, you can freeze it or use it to fill Amandines, page 12). Jiggle the crust a bit to even out the ganache, and leave the tart on the counter until the filling sets, about 20 minutes, depending on the temperature of your kitchen. (If your kitchen is really warm, pop the tart into the refrigerator for 20 minutes, just to set the ganache, then keep it at room temperature after it has set.)

KEEPING: The tart is best served at room temperature the day it is made. If you must keep it, refrigerate it overnight, then let it stand at room temperature for about 2 hours before serving.

AN AMERICAN IN PARIS: I love this tart straight up, solo, on its own, but a little bit of whipped crème fraîche (see page 50) or heavy cream never hurts, nor does a drizzle of melted best-quality vanilla ice cream— think of it as instant crème anglaise.

8 ounces (225 grams) bittersweet chocolate, finely chopped

⅔ cup (160 grams) heavy cream

2 large egg yolks, at room temperature

2 tablespoons (1 ounce; 30 grams) unsalted butter, at room temperature

½ moist, plump vanilla bean, split lengthwise

1 fully baked 6½-inch (16-cm) tart shell made from Sweet Tart Dough (page 180)

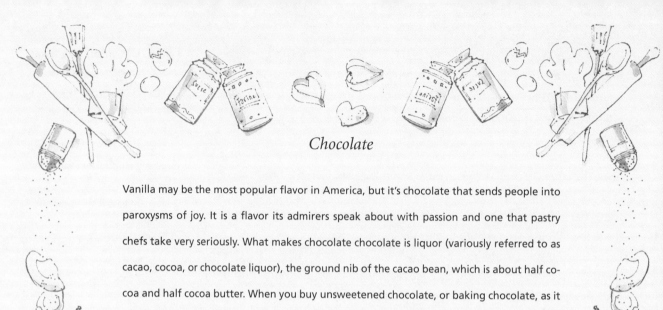

Chocolate

Vanilla may be the most popular flavor in America, but it's chocolate that sends people into paroxysms of joy. It is a flavor its admirers speak about with passion and one that pastry chefs take very seriously. What makes chocolate chocolate is liquor (variously referred to as cacao, cocoa, or chocolate liquor), the ground nib of the cacao bean, which is about half cocoa and half cocoa butter. When you buy unsweetened chocolate, or baking chocolate, as it is sometimes called, you get 100 percent chocolate liquor. All other chocolates—bittersweet, semisweet, milk, and imported white—are a blend of sugar, often additional cocoa butter, and sometimes cocoa powder. Since what gives chocolate its chocolateness is the liquor, it stands to reason that the greater the percentage of cacao, the more chocolatey and less sweet the chocolate will be. The trick is to know the percentage of chocolate liquor in your chocolate—not such an easy trick in America, where it is not a requirement, as it is in France, to display the percentage of liquor on the label. Here the Food and Drug Administration stipulates that bittersweet and semisweet chocolates (the FDA does not distinguish between the two) must contain a minimum of 35 percent cocoa liquor. However, pastry chefs in Paris usually use chocolates with a minimum of 60 percent cocoa and very often opt for chocolates that have 70 percent cocoa liquor or more. If you want to select your chocolates by the numbers, I suggest you choose French chocolates by Valrhona (see the Source Guide, page 185), the choice of many Paris pastry chefs, or if you'd like an American chocolate, choose Scharffen Berger (see the Source Guide), a very fine chocolate and the first American brand to include cacao percentages on its labels.

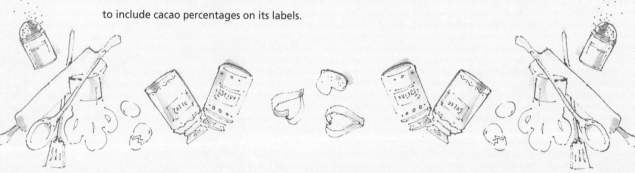

A Chocolate Tart for Sonia Rykiel / Tarte au Chocolat pour Sonia Rykiel

Adapted from Christian Constant

Sonia Rykiel, the internationally renowned clothing designer, is a celebrated devotee of chocolate and a member of Le Club des Croquers de Chocolat *(The Chocolate Connoisseurs' Club), a select group of chocolate obsessives. It was for Madame Rykiel that another of its dedicated members, Christian Constant (see page 108), one of Paris's premier chocolatiers, created this tart, which is simple but as dazzling as any of Rykiel's designs. The tart is filled with chocolate ganache and topped with a sunburst of sliced bananas, one of Sonia Rykiel's favorite fruits and, with chocolate, one of the world's best flavor combinations.*

8 ounces (230 grams) bittersweet chocolate, finely chopped

1 cup (250 grams) heavy cream

4 tablespoons (2 ounces; 60 grams) unsalted butter, cut into 4 pieces, at room temperature

1 fully baked 8-inch (20-cm) tart shell made from Sweet Tart Dough (page 180)

½ cup (150 grams) apricot jam, strained

2 to 3 ripe but firm bananas

Fresh lemon juice (optional)

1. Put the chocolate in a heatproof bowl. Pour the heavy cream into a small saucepan, bring to a full boil, pour it over the chocolate, and let the mixture rest for 30 seconds. Using a whisk, very gently stir until the chocolate is melted and smooth, then whisk in the butter until melted.

2. Pour the ganache into the baked tart shell, taking care not to overfill the crust. Refrigerate to firm and chill the ganache, about 2 hours. (*The tart can be covered with plastic wrap and kept refrigerated overnight. If you have ganache left over, you can cool it, pack it airtight, and keep it in the freezer for up to 1 month; or use it to fill Amandines, page 12, or to top Tiger Tea Cakes, page 118.*)

3. Shortly before serving, bring the apricot jam to the boil in a saucepan over medium heat; or do this in a microwave oven. Keep the jam warm.

4. Peel the bananas and cut them on a slight diagonal into slices that are a scant ¼ inch (5 mm) thick. (M. Constant warns that if the slices are too thin, the bananas will darken very quickly. If you are concerned about the bananas blackening, you can toss them with a squirt or two of lemon juice. It will add another taste to the tart, but it will preserve their color.) Starting at the edge of the tart, arrange the bananas in concentric circles, slightly overlapping the slices in each circle and having each circle slightly overlap the preceding circle. Brush the bananas with the hot apricot jam, glazing them evenly. The tart can

be served as soon as the glaze is cool (about 10 minutes), or you can allow it to remain at room temperature a little longer to soften the ganache.

KEEPING: The crust filled with ganache can be refrigerated overnight; however, once the bananas are added to the tart, it should be served within a couple of hours.

AN AMERICAN IN PARIS: If you love bananas, you will love my variation on this superb tart—it has bananas inside and out. Before you fill the shell with ganache, peel and cut 1 or 2 bananas on the diagonal into ¼-inch-thick (7 mm-thick) slices. Melt 1 to 2 tablespoons (15 to 30 grams) unsalted butter in a skillet over high heat and add 2 tablespoons (25 grams) sugar; when the sugar is lightly caramelized, toss in the bananas. Still working over high heat, sauté the bananas to caramelize them. Using a slotted spoon, transfer the bananas to a plate to cool. When they are cool, pat off any excess butter with paper towels and lay the bananas in the tart shell before pouring in the ganache. Chill, then finish with the top layer of bananas.

Baked Apple Tart / Tarte aux Pommes au Four

Adapted from Dalloyau

This tart from Dalloyau (see page 144), whose pâtisseries and salons de thé epitomize luxe, calme, et volupté, *can finish an elegant little dinner party or cap a casual Sunday supper. It can be served at teatime or be enjoyed as a midnight snack. And it can bring smiles to grown-ups and kids alike. In part, it owes its tremendous appeal to the apples, which are caramelized stovetop and then baked through in the oven. But it is the combination of these apples, the thin layer of lightly nutty almond cream they sit on, the crunchy crust that holds everything together, and the grated apples strewn across the top (a surprisingly rustic touch from very urbane Dalloyau) that gives this tart a special place in the universe of wonderfully good French apple tarts, a universe that also includes Toast-Point Apple Tart (page 74) and Tea-Flavored Tarte Tatin (page 78).*

THE ALMOND CREAM

1½ tablespoons (¾ ounce; 20 grams) unsalted butter, at room temperature

1 tablespoon sugar

¼ cup (30 grams) ground almonds

1 large egg, preferably at room temperature

2 tablespoons (30 grams) heavy cream

1 tablespoon Calvados or apple brandy (or 1 tablespoon pure vanilla extract)

1. **TO MAKE THE CREAM:** Working in a medium bowl with a whisk, beat the butter and sugar together for a minute or so, until the sugar dissolves and the butter whitens a little. Whisk in the almonds, then the egg, beating until the mixture is blended. Finally, whisk in the cream and Calvados. Cover the bowl and refrigerate until needed. *(The cream can be kept covered in the refrigerator for up to 3 days.)*

2. **TO MAKE THE APPLES:** Center a rack in the oven and preheat the oven to 350°F (180°C).

3. Cut 4 of the apples in half and slice each half into thirds. Grate the remaining 2 apples on the coarse side of a box grater.

4. Melt 1 tablespoon of the butter and 1 tablespoon of the sugar in a large skillet over high heat. Add the grated apples and cook, stirring, until they are golden brown, about 3 minutes. Using a slotted spoon, transfer the apples to a plate. Add the remaining 6 tablespoons (85 grams) butter and the rest of the sugar to the pan and, when the butter is bubbling, toss in the apple slices. Cook the apples, stirring frequently, until they are lightly caramelized, 5 to 7 minutes. Pour in the Calvados, turn off the heat, and carefully touch a match to the liquid. When the flames die down, pull the pan from the stove.

5. Transfer the apple slices to a baking pan (or keep them in the skillet if it is ovenproof) and bake for 20 minutes, or until they are almost cooked through. Cool for 30 minutes.

6. **TO ASSEMBLE THE TART:** Position a rack in the lower third of the oven and preheat the oven to 350°F (180°C). Line a rimmed baking sheet with parchment paper and put the tart shell on the sheet.

7. Spoon the almond cream evenly into the crust. Top with the baked apples, arranging them attractively in a single layer. Check the grated apples—if they are wet, press them either between your palms or between paper towels. Fluff up the grated apples with your fingers or a fork and arrange them over the apple slices, leaving a bare border of an inch (2.5 cm) or so.

8. Bake the tart for 40 to 50 minutes, or until the almond cream has puffed and the apples are beautifully browned. Cool the tart on a rack; unmold and serve it when it is either just warm or at room temperature. Dust the tart generously with confectioners' sugar right before bringing it to the table.

KEEPING: While all of the elements can be prepared ahead, once the tart is assembled, it should be baked immediately, and once it is baked, it should be served soon thereafter.

AN AMERICAN IN PARIS: This tart is perfect on its own and delicious with either a bit of crème fraîche (see page 50) or vanilla crème anglaise, but the American in me loves it with a fat scoop of vanilla ice cream.

THE APPLES

6 large apples (2¼ pounds; 1 kilo), preferably Fuji or Granny Smith, peeled and cored

7 tablespoons (3½ ounces; 100 grams) unsalted butter

⅓ cup sugar (75 grams)

2 tablespoons Calvados or apple brandy (or 1½ tablespoons pure vanilla extract)

THE CRUST

1 unbaked 9-inch (24-cm) tart shell made from puff pastry (homemade, page 182, or store-bought) or Sweet Tart Dough (page 180)

Confectioners' sugar to finish

Of Tarts and Dough

A Parisian friend of mine, a wonderful woman who has earned her reputation as a hostess less for her culinary skills than for her considerable grace, dazzled me one evening with a pear tart in a crust that defined perfection. I wouldn't have dreamed of being so rude as to compliment her tart in such a way as to make it clear that I was surprised by the crust's delicacy, but I did say it was delicious and slipped in a comment about the crust's lovely texture. All I got in return was a hostessly thank-you and the admission that she, too, liked the dessert, in good measure because it was foolproof. Foolproof? Maybe I had underestimated her kitchen witchery. It wasn't until years later, when I was living and cooking in Paris, that I understood just how foolproof her recipe was. She, like the majority of Paris home cooks—*moi* now included—thinks nothing of making tarts, sweet or savory, mostly because she doesn't have to think about making the crust: every corner market sells high-quality ready-made, already-rolled-out dough. You can buy pizza dough, *pâte brisée* (a sugarless dough for savory tarts), *pâte sablée* (a sweet tart dough), and all-butter puff pastry as easily as you can a dozen eggs.

Here, at home, it is not as easy to find the variety or, sadly, the quality of ready-made crusts available in France. This is particularly true if you're looking for the equivalent of *pâte sablée*. Most ready-made doughs found in the freezer compartments of supermarkets are made with nary a pat of butter. But that doesn't mean you must start from scratch with every tart. Seek and ye shall find exceptionally good ready-to-roll puff pastry. (I'm thinking of all-butter Dufour Pastry Kitchen puff pastry dough; see the Source Guide, page 185). You can use puff pastry for any tart, sweet or savory—it will do nothing but make the tart more elegant.

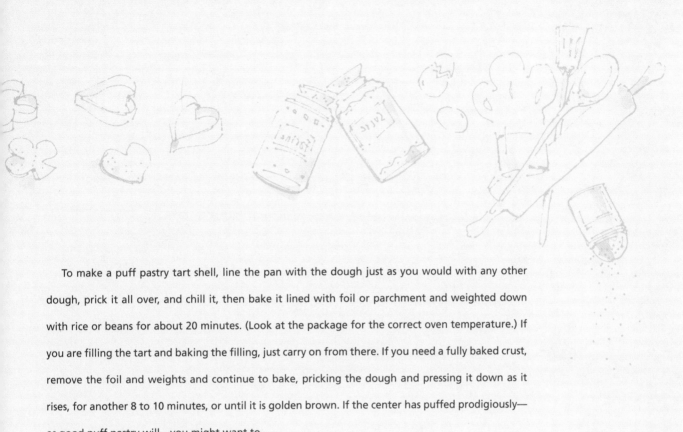

To make a puff pastry tart shell, line the pan with the dough just as you would with any other dough, prick it all over, and chill it, then bake it lined with foil or parchment and weighted down with rice or beans for about 20 minutes. (Look at the package for the correct oven temperature.) If you are filling the tart and baking the filling, just carry on from there. If you need a fully baked crust, remove the foil and weights and continue to bake, pricking the dough and pressing it down as it rises, for another 8 to 10 minutes, or until it is golden brown. If the center has puffed prodigiously— as good puff pastry will—you might want to poke the big bubbles and toss away the resulting shards.

LENÔTRE One of the great thrills of my professional life was attending Gaston Lenôtre's eightieth birthday party on May 25, 2000, in Paris. Granted, it was a celebration for hundreds of people, but when the invitation arrived, I was as excited as Cinderella going to the ball. Of course, unlike Cinderella, I didn't care about Prince Charming. I just wanted to meet the man who, unbeknownst to him, had directed my career toward pastry.

My story is a minor one compared to those of the thousands of chefs who call Gaston Lenôtre their mentor. I credit Lenôtre's first cookbook, *Lenôtre's Desserts and Pastries*, with teaching me to bake, and his school, where I took classes alongside chefs from around the world, with solidifying my passion for the profession.

But Lenôtre did so much more than get me started—he started a pastry revolution. In much the same way that Escoffier modernized French cuisine, Lenôtre modernized pastry by developing a way to produce his pastries, and later the foods for his catering business, in one facility and in large quantity without giving up an iota of quality. In addition, he created a school, really a university and research laboratory, to develop new techniques and products and to pass along the field's savoir-faire to the more than one thousand people who work under the name Lenôtre, to other professionals, and, most recently, to amateurs too.

These days, Lenôtre is a big brand name, associated with seven Paris boutiques; three restaurants, including Le Pré Catalan in the Bois de Boulogne and Le Panoramique in the Stade de France, the huge sports arena minutes from Paris; thirty-four sales points throughout the world; the school, École Lenôtre, just outside Paris; and a boutique in the Paris Hotel in Las Vegas. Not bad for a Normandy farm boy whose first thirteen years as a student and young pastry chef were marked by family illness, economic depression, and World War II.

I know all of this because I am fascinated by what Lenôtre has done. But you don't need to know any of this to become a fan. For you, one little almond *tuile*, a classic cookie shaped like a French roof tile; an *éclat framboise*, a chocolate-raspberry cake topped with a sleek square of bittersweet chocolate set at a jaunty angle; a triangle of the heart-warming Toast-Point Apple Tart (page 74); an impeccable brioche; a small cup of mousse; or a grand box of artfully crafted candies will win you over.

All of these sweets, as well as Lenôtre's grand classics, including the Concorde, a chocolate meringue extravaganza, and the Casino, a vanilla Bavarian cream cake trimmed with jammy jelly-roll slices, were passed out to the birthday well-wishers who gathered at the Trocadero Gardens. The view from the Trocadero is magnificent, encompassing fountains and the Eiffel Tower from base to tip. That day it also included a view of Gaston Lenôtre's birthday cake, which was thirty feet tall and, until it was time to sing *"Bon Anniversaire,"* a work in progress: eighty pastry cooks were lined up along the cake's layers, finishing the decorations, which depicted every aspect of the honoree's life. The cake was spectacular, and pictures of it appeared in newspapers and magazines for weeks after the party. But pictures are all that remain of the cake. As committed as M. Lenôtre is to teaching, there are no plans to include the towering confection in any of his forthcoming cookbooks.

Toast-Point Apple Tart /

Tarte aux Pommes au Pain de Mie

Adapted from Lenôtre

The first time I spied this apple tart in one of the several Lenôtre shops in Paris (see page 72), I was delighted. It was the most unusual apple tart I had ever seen and it turned out to be one of the best I have ever eaten. It was as though Lenôtre's creative genie, Gérard Gautheron, had decided to make a tart that would embrace all the apple-friendly flavors we love—and then added a fillip or two more just for fun. The apples in the tart are quickly cooked in butter, then given a last-minute sugar-and-vanilla shower. But the fun begins when the caramelized apples are laid in their sweet tart crust, because that's when the butter-and-brown-sugar toast points are propped up between the sliced fruit, the apples covered with a luscious caramel cream, and the assemblage strewn with raisins and walnut pieces. Consider the tart a tasty gift from Fantasyland.

THE APPLES

2 pounds (900 grams) Golden Delicious apples (about 4)

2 tablespoons (1 ounce; 30 grams) unsalted butter

2 tablespoons (25 grams) sugar

Pulp of ¼ vanilla bean

THE TOAST

2 tablespoons (1 ounce; 30 grams) unsalted butter, at room temperature

½ tablespoon (23 grams) packed light brown sugar

4 slices firm white bread or country bread (if the crusts are hard, remove them)

1. **TO MAKE THE APPLES:** Peel, quarter, and core the apples, then cut each quarter in half. Melt the butter in a large skillet over medium-high heat, and when the bubbles subside, toss in the apple slices. Cook and stir until the apples are lightly browned and almost cooked through, about 10 minutes. Sprinkle over the sugar and vanilla pulp and continue to cook and stir until the sugar caramelizes the apples, about 5 minutes more. Using a slotted spoon, transfer the apples to a plate and allow them to cool to room temperature. *(If necessary, you can make the apples up to 6 hours ahead; keep them lightly covered at room temperature.)*

2. **TO MAKE THE TOAST:** Preheat the broiler (or do this in a toaster oven). Using a flexible rubber spatula, beat the butter and sugar together until well blended.

3. Spread the butter on one side of each piece of bread. Place the bread buttered side up on a nonstick baking sheet and toast the bread under the broiler. Turn the bread over and toast the other side. Cut each slice of bread in half on the diagonal and set aside to cool to room temperature.

4. **TO MAKE THE CARAMEL CREAM:** Bring the heavy cream to a full boil in a saucepan over heat (or do this in a microwave oven). Meanwhile, working in a large measuring cup with a spout or in a medium bowl, beat the egg, egg yolks, sugar, and vanilla pulp together with a whisk until the mixture thickens and pales slightly.

5. Whisking gently all the while (you need to be gentle so you don't create bubbles), gradually mix the hot cream into the eggs. If the cream is bubbly, skim the bubbles from the cream, then rap the measuring cup or bowl against the counter, just to make sure all the bubbles are gone.

6. **TO FINISH:** Center a rack in the oven and preheat the oven to 325°F (165°C). Line an insulated baking sheet with parchment paper or stack two regular baking sheets and line the top sheet with parchment. The idea is to give the tart gentle heat.

7. The best way to assemble this tart is to line up the apple slices in parallel rows in the tart shell: have one row support the next, and have all the slices face the same direction. When the apples are in place, arrange the toast triangles decoratively among the slices, with the broad base of the toast against the crust and the points up. Scatter over the walnuts and raisins and pour in about one-third to one-half of the caramel cream. (If you try to pour in all the cream now, it will spill over.)

8. Carefully slide the baking sheet(s) into the oven and bake the tart for 10 minutes, at which point the cream should be set enough for you to pour in enough of the remaining cream to come up to the rim of the tart. (You may have some cream left over.) Continue baking for another 40 to 45 minutes (total baking time: 50 to 55 minutes), or until a knife inserted into the cream at the center of the tart comes out clean. (The cream should shimmy the way a quiche filling does.) Transfer the tart, still on its baking sheet(s), to a cooling rack and allow to rest until it is just warm, when it is at its best, about 30 minutes.

KEEPING: While you can make each of the tart's elements a few hours ahead, once the tart is baked, it should be served the day it is made, preferably while it is still warm.

AN AMERICAN IN PARIS: As though this tart weren't whimsical enough, I often play around with it and replace the white bread with slices of cinnamon-swirl raisin bread.

THE CARAMEL CREAM

1¼ cups (315 grams) heavy cream
1 large egg
3 large egg yolks
⅓ cup (65 grams) sugar
Pulp of ¼ vanilla bean

THE CRUST

1 partially baked 10-inch (26-cm) tart
    shell made from Sweet Tart
    Dough (page 180)

TO FINISH

2 tablespoons (20 grams) walnut
    pieces
2 tablespoons (20 grams) moist,
    plump golden raisins

MARIAGE FRÈRES

One drizzly morning, I sat with Kitti Cha Sangmanee, president and tea taster for Mariage Frères, France's most cherished tea purveyor, and Franck Desains, the company's general director and designer, sipping deeply aromatic Opium Hill tea, the first tea to come from what was once an opium field bordering Burma and Thailand, and talking about Paris, its way of life, its wonders, and its infinite capacity to surprise. It was Kitti Cha who said that what he loved about Paris was its secrets, the unknowns that waited to be discovered behind closed doors. "So much of Paris," he said, "is hidden. You can never be sure what you will find when you push back any of the heavy doors that keep the intimate Paris from view." He might have been talking about the doors to the Mariage Frères boutiques and tearooms, for as beckoning as each is on the outside, it is only when you enter that the full breadth of its elegance is revealed.

Whether you go to the Mariage Frères mother house in the heart of the art-and-boutique-filled Le Marais, to the shop in the sixth *arrondissement* near the Seine, or to the one on the rue du Faubourg Saint-Honoré, a short stroll from the Arc de Triomphe, the experience is similar—you are transported to a place of serenity, a sensuous oasis, an environment in which, as Kitti Cha says, "you can travel in your mind."

Each Mariage Frères boutique houses a shop, a museum, and a *salon de thé.* The shops sell an exquisite array of teapots; tea-flavored cookies, jellies, and chocolates; tea-scented candles; and, of course, teas, more than four hundred kinds, which are grown exclusively for Mariage Frères, selected by their tea men, and blended *à la maison,* just as it has always been done.

The Mariage brothers have been tea men since the mid-1600s, only bringing their tea business to rue Bourg-Tibourg in Paris in 1854. Here the brothers sold tea wholesale, blending the teas on the wooden counters that are still used by Mariage Frères today. It was not until 1984 that Mariage Frères began selling tea retail, and when they did, they developed the tea museums, ensuring that everything that came before 1984 would be lovingly preserved and enchantingly presented.

It was also after 1984 that the Rive Gauche and Étoile boutiques were opened and that the *salons de thé* were established. In many ways, it is within the tearooms that the true *French* art of tea can best be appreciated. Each Mariage Frères *salon de thé* is a cocoon of calm. Tea is always served in a perfect pot, brewed to the perfect strength, and offered at the perfect temperature. At lunch, the dishes are tea-accented and the gracious waiters are ready to recommend the right tea to accompany each course. When you return late in the afternoon for tea and a sweet, you find that, like the savory midday dishes, the pastries are tea-flavored. Depending on the day, there may be madeleines with Earl Grey tea and honey (page 20), *tarte Tatin* flavored with vanilla tea (page 78), or *financiers* with green tea. But no matter whether the dessert cart is laden with fruit tarts or fancy cookies, whether you come for lunch or a morning pastry, or whether you slip into the salon for a solitary moment and cup of a tea as restorative as the house's jasmine pearl, you are sure to feel cosseted, as I always do, and bound, as I often am, to find yourself doing just what Kitti Cha Sangmanee said you would, "traveling in your mind." It is as though the tea you savor in this quiet place had been blended with a spoonful of magic.

Tea-Flavored Tarte Tatin /

Tarte Tatin au Thé

Adapted from Mariage Frères

My editor, Jennifer Josephy, loves this tart and insisted that I run to Mariage Frères (see page 76) to taste it—a delightful assignment, but not one that was easily achieved since, like most of the sweets served at the Mariage Frères tea salons, it makes intermittent guest appearances when the season and the chef's whim are in sync. I got lucky one afternoon and, with my first bite, understood why Jennifer wanted me to beg for the recipe: by infusing the tart's butter with their exquisite vanilla tea, the team at Mariage Frères had done the impossible—they'd improved on what seemed like an already perfect recipe.

Tarte Tatin is a recipe with a story. History has it that the Tatin sisters, proprietors of a boardinghouse in Sologne, slid their apple tart into the oven and only then realized they'd forgotten to line the pan with a crust. Not wanting to waste the apples, they covered them with a piece of dough and, when all was baked, turned the tart upside down and served it—no doubt with a "Voilà." But tarte Tatin *is also a recipe with a mystique. People talk about the most memorable* tarte Tatin *they have ever had, and bakers talk about the intricacies of making it. Call*

me silly, but I think a tarte Tatin *is one of the easiest big-deal desserts to make. Maybe this is because I made my first (quite fabulous) tarte Tatin when I didn't know it was supposed to be tricky. True, there are some little ambiguities in every Tatin recipe, but they're just that, little, and, better yet, the recipe is forgiving.*

The trickiest thing about a tarte Tatin *is that it's an upside-down affair, so you can't look at the tart and know that it's done. I'm not sure why this never disturbed the American home bakers of the 1950s, who were making pineapple upside-down cakes for weekly bridge games without giving their upside-downness a second thought. However, as long as you bake the pastry long enough, you needn't worry, since the apples, which are almost cooked through before the pastry is rolled over them, will surely be done—and characteristically caramelized—by the time the crust is golden brown and flaky.*

A word on measurements: *Here's the ambiguity—the number of apples you'll need will depend on the size of your apples, the size of your pan (see Step 1), and whether you want a single or double layer of apples (see Step 4). Stay flexible. Buy a couple more apples than you think you'll need, and peel and core them as you go. Remember, the original* tarte Tatin *was an accident. This is a dessert to enjoy, not one to obsess over.*

1. The tart can be made in a *tarte Tatin* pan (available in specialty shops), or a 9- to 10-inch (24- to 26-cm) cast-iron skillet (a great pan for this tart), or other heavy, ovenproof skillet. (This is not a recipe that demands extraordinary precision. If you've got a pan that is slightly larger or slightly smaller, you can adjust the number of apples by eye as you go along.) Working on a well-floured counter, roll out the puff pastry until it is ⅛ inch (3 mm) thick, then cut out a round that is about 1 inch (2.5 cm) larger in diameter than the pan you'll be using. Slide the rolled-out dough onto a parchment-lined baking sheet, prick it all over with the tines of a fork or the tip of a paring knife, cover with plastic wrap, and chill until needed. *(The dough can remain in the refrigerator for 1 day.)*

2. Line a sieve with a single layer of moistened cheesecloth and set the sieve over a bowl. Melt the butter in a small saucepan, then pull the pan from the heat and stir in the tea and vanilla extract. Allow the tea to infuse for 1 minute, then strain the flavored butter into the bowl; discard the tea leaves.

About 8 ounces (240 grams) puff pastry, homemade (page 182) or store-bought (see the Source Guide, page 185)

1 stick (4 ounces; 115 grams) unsalted butter

2 tablespoons (15 grams) vanilla tea, preferably Vanille Impériale from Mariage Frères (see the Source Guide)

1 teaspoon pure vanilla extract

¾ cup (150 grams) sugar

6 to 8 medium apples, preferably a sweet firm apple such as Gala or Golden Delicious, peeled, cored, and quartered

3. Center a rack in the oven and preheat the oven to 375°F (190°C). Line a baking sheet with parchment paper and set it aside.

4. Use a pastry brush to cover the sides of the tart pan with some of the vanilla butter, then coat the sides with some of the sugar. Pour the remaining butter into the pan and sprinkle the remaining sugar over the butter. Arrange a single layer of apples, rounded (peeled) side down, in closely packed concentric circles. The apples will shrink as they cook, so make sure to get as snug a fit as you can. It might be necessary to custom-cut a few of the apple quarters to fill odd spaces. If you want a second layer of apples (a second layer will give you a higher tart), cut the remaining apple quarters lengthwise in half (or peel and core as many additional apples as you need and cut the apples into eighths) and build another layer with them. Don't worry about arranging them neatly—this layer will never be seen.

5. Set the pan over medium heat and cook until the sugar caramelizes to a deep golden brown color, about 20 minutes. (Don't go too far from the stove—you may have to adjust the heat to keep the sugar from burning.) Pull the pan from the heat and place it on the parchment-lined baking sheet.

6. Using a wooden spoon, press down gently on the apples and, if necessary, nudge them a bit to fill any gaps you see. Put the puff pastry circle over the apples, tucking the edges in very loosely. When you tuck, you may have to double the pastry over on itself, and that's OK. It's also OK if some of the pastry overlaps the rim of the pan; it will shrink to the right size as it bakes. Slide the baking sheet into the oven and bake the tart for 30 to 40 minutes, or until the pastry is puffed and, most important, golden.

7. Moving with speed and conviction—this isn't an operation for a timid slowpoke—cover the pan with a large serving plate and invert the tart onto the plate; remove the pan. If any of the apples have stuck to the pan (as some usually will), gently loosen them from the pan with a small metal spatula and reunite them with their companions. Allow the tart to cool for 10 minutes or so before serving, or wait until it is only just warm.

KEEPING: There's no holding onto this tart. It should be served within an hour or so of emerging from the oven.

AN AMERICAN IN PARIS: I've been known to go an extra step on this recipe and do as my Paris friend Suzy "Born to Shop" Gershman does—toss a few pecans into the bottom of the pan before arranging the apples over the butter and sugar. Think of it as fusion cuisine.

Cherry Clafoutis / Clafoutis aux Cerises

Adapted from Pâtisserie Mulot

Among my Paris apartment's many assets is its proximity to Gérard Mulot's pastry shop (see page 102): I can walk there in five minutes flat—and do so often. Pass by the shop and you might find me, surrounded by like-minded admirers, marveling at the tarts topped with arrangements to rival any fruit-filled cornucopia painted by Caravaggio. Yet, as stunning as these tarts are, the tart that consistently sells out is M. Mulot's simplest tart, his clafoutis. In fact, the tart is so popular he makes it three times a day, the better to ensure that its crust is crisp and its filling custardy, morning, noon, or night.

The traditional clafoutis is a specialty of the Limousin region of France, where it is always made with fresh cherries and almost always with unpitted cherries, since the pits are thought to give the fruit more flavor. This clafoutis strays from tradition in that it is baked in a crust (the original was crustless, which could explain why the French Academy declared it a cake rather than a tart) and studded with griottes, small ruby-colored sour cherries. Griottes are available frozen (M. Mulot's preference) or jarred at specialty shops. They are also often seen imported from Italy, packed in syrup in blue-and-white-patterned milk-glass bottles. However, as good as these Italian griottes are, they are OK but not ideal for this tart because of their heavy syrup. If you cannot find griottes either frozen or jarred, stick with tradition: make this clafoutis with fresh cherries, pitted or not.

1. Center a rack in the oven and preheat the oven to 400°F (200°C). Put the tart shell on a parchment-lined baking sheet and keep the setup on the counter.

2. Whisk the eggs in a mixing bowl just until they are blended. Whisk in the sugar, followed by the crème fraîche (go easy on the crème fraîche—beat it too energetically, and you'll have whipped cream) and the vanilla. Switch to a rubber spatula and gently stir the cherries into the batter.

3. Turn the batter into the crust, poke the cherries around a bit if necessary so that they're more or less evenly distributed, and slide the baking sheet into the oven. (If you have too much batter for the tart, as might be the case if you are using heavy cream, pour in just enough to fill the tart and bake for 10 minutes, then pour in as much of the remaining batter as possible; continue baking as directed.) Bake for about 25 minutes, or until the custard is set at the center—tap the tart pan, and the custard shouldn't jiggle. Transfer the clafoutis to a cooling rack. You can serve the clafoutis after it has cooled for about 15 minutes (the temperature at which Gérard Mulot prefers his clafoutis), or you can allow it to come to room temperature.

KEEPING: The clafoutis will keep for about 12 hours at room temperature. It is best served shortly after it is made and is always best unchilled.

AN AMERICAN IN PARIS: I've made this clafoutis with winy dried cherries and loved it—the tangy dried cherries are wonderful with the rich custard filling. But before you plop the dried cherries into the tart shell, make sure they're moist and plump. If they're not, steam them for a minute or two, then pat them dry before proceeding. Of course, you can also make this tart with poached (or high-quality canned) apricots or peaches, purple prune plums, or an assortment of raspberries, blackberries, and blueberries.

1 partially baked 9-inch (24-cm) tart shell made from Sweet Tart Dough (page 180)

3 large eggs

6 tablespoons (75 grams) sugar

1 cup (240 grams) crème fraîche, homemade (page 50) or store-bought, or heavy cream

Pulp of ½ moist, plump vanilla bean or 2 teaspoons pure vanilla extract

11 ounces (330 grams) frozen griottes or sour cherries, defrosted and patted dry, or sour or sweet fresh cherries, pitted or not (see headnote)

Whole-Lemon Tart / Tarte au Citron

Adapted from Rollet-Pradier

At Rollet-Pradier (see page 158), the pâtisserie and salon de thé just behind the Assemblée Nationale and the Musée d'Orsay, they know what lemon lovers are looking for—tang—and they've created a tart that takes tang seriously. The signature Rollet-Pradier lemon tart contains just one lemon, but it contains every bit of that lemon except the seeds, so you get the powerful flavor of the zest as well as the jolting freshness of the juice and pulp. Since there is little but sugar, egg, and melted butter to soften these bold flavors, the tart is both audacious and instantly appealing.

1. Center a rack in the oven and preheat the oven to 325°F (165°C). Line a rimmed baking sheet with parchment paper and put the tart shell on the sheet.

2. Slice the lemon into thin wedges, remove the seeds, and toss the lemon and sugar into the container of a blender or food processor. Blend or process, scraping down the sides of the container as needed, until the lemon is thoroughly puréed and blended with the sugar, 1 to 2 minutes. Turn the mixture into a bowl and, using a whisk, gently stir in the whole egg and the yolk, followed by the cornstarch and melted butter. Pour the filling into the crust.

3. Slide the baking sheet into the oven and bake the tart for 20 minutes. Increase the oven temperature to 350°F (180°C) and bake for another 15 to 20 minutes, or until the filling is bubbling and lightly browned. Transfer the tart, still on the baking sheet, to a cooling rack and allow it to cool for at least 20 minutes before removing it from the pan. The tart is ready to be served when it reaches room temperature.

KEEPING: The tart is best served the day it is made, but, if necessary, it can be kept in the refrigerator overnight; bring to cool room temperature before serving.

AN AMERICAN IN PARIS: For a change of tang, make this tart with a couple of Key limes, or try it with a regular, always-available lime *ordinaire.*

1 partially baked 9-inch (24-cm) tart shell made from Sweet Tart Dough (page 180)

1 average-sized lemon (about 4½ ounces; 130 grams), rinsed and dried

1½ cups (300 grams) sugar

1 large egg

1 large egg yolk

1½ tablespoons (12 grams) cornstarch

1 stick (4 ounces; 115 grams) unsalted butter, melted and cooled

Fig and Citrus Tart / Tarte aux Figues et Agrumes

Adapted from Fauchon

A week or so after powwowing with the people at Fauchon, Paris's most cele-brated gourmet shop and pastry shrine (see page 128), about which of their spe-cialties to feature in this book, my fax machine burbled and out came the recipes we'd decided on—and one more: this remarkable tart. As soon as I read through the recipe, I knew I would love it, and so I couldn't decide what to do. Should I call, ask if it was a mistake, and risk having them withdraw it? Or should I just go along my merry way, operating under the presumed protection of ignorance? What I did was call to thank them for sending such terrific recipes, and then I ca-sually mentioned that I was surprised to see a recipe for a fig and citrus tart. Well, I was even more surprised when I learned that it had been included at the insis-tence of Fauchon's president, who has a soft spot for this indulgence and didn't want American pastry lovers to be deprived of its pleasures. Merci mille fois, M. le Président.

The most uncommon part of this tart is its filling, a riff on the pâtissier's stan-dard almond cream. Here the cream is flavored—and, as a consequence, tex-tured—with the honey-sweet seedy pulp of dried figs. It is a brilliant addition to the cream. The tart is made even more delectable by being topped with just-slightly tangy segments of red grapefruit, plump slices of navel orange, and wedges of fresh figs. It is not a combination that springs readily to mind, but then Fauchon did not build its reputa-tion on the ordinary.

THE CITRUS FRUIT

2 navel oranges

1 Ruby Red grapefruit

1. **TO PREPARE THE CITRUS:** With a knife, peel the oranges and grapefruit down to the fruit, then run the knife along the connective membranes to release the segments of fruit. Place the segments between triple layers of paper towels and let them dry for at least 1 hour or, if you have the time, overnight.

2. **TO PREPARE THE FIG CREAM:** Bring a small pot of water to the boil, toss in the figs, and pull the pan from the heat. Let the figs soak for about 30 minutes.

3. When the figs are soft and plump, drain them, pat them dry, and cut each one crosswise in half. Using a small spoon, scrape out the seedy pulp from each half. (If you get a little of the outer skin as well, don't worry.) Discard the skin.

4. Put the butter in the bowl of a mixer fitted with the paddle attachment and beat on medium speed until it is soft but not fluffy. (At no point do you want to beat air into this cream.) Reduce the mixer speed to low and, one by one, mix in the figs, confectioners' sugar, potato starch, ground almonds, egg, and, finally, the kirsch. Switch to a rubber spatula and fold in the whipped cream. Cover and chill for about 1 hour. *(The fig cream can be made up to 1 day ahead and kept tightly covered in the refrigerator.)*

5. **TO FINISH:** Center a rack in the oven and preheat the oven to 350°F (180°C). Place the tart pan on a parchment-lined baking sheet.

6. Cutting from top to bottom, slice each purple fig into 5 pieces. Spoon the fig cream into the tart shell and smooth the top with an offset spatula. Arrange the orange, grapefruit, and fig slices in a decorative pattern (concentric circles are classic and attractive) over the top of the tart. Don't cover every bit of the fig cream—it will bubble and rise as it bakes, and it's nice to leave space for it to bubble up around the fruit.

7. Slide the baking sheet into the oven and bake the tart for 50 to 60 minutes, or until the cream has risen and turned golden brown. If you slip a knife into the cream, it should come out clean. Transfer the tart to a rack and cool to room temperature. Dust with confectioners' sugar just before serving.

KEEPING: While the citrus fruit and fig cream can be made up to 1 day ahead, the finished tart should be served—at room temperature or just slightly chilled—the day it is made.

AN AMERICAN IN PARIS: No sooner did I make this filling than I wanted to find a hundred other ways to use it. Here's one of my favorites, a variation on the French classic *bostook,* a clever and delicious way to use stale bread: Cut slices of day-old brioche, challah, or another type of egg bread, or even croissants, as though you were making sandwiches. Place the bread on a parchment-lined baking sheet and spread each slice with fig cream, leaving a slim border bare. Sprinkle the cream with sliced almonds and bake in a preheated 350°F (180°C) oven for about 10 minutes, or until the fig cream is puffed and starting to brown and the bread crusts are golden. Cool before serving.

THE FIG CREAM

5½ ounces (145 grams) dried figs (about 7)

3 tablespoons (1½ ounces; 45 grams) unsalted butter, at room temperature

Slightly rounded ⅓ cup (45 grams) confectioners' sugar, sifted

1½ teaspoons potato starch (available in the baking or kosher foods section of most supermarkets), sifted

½ cup (55 grams) ground blanched almonds

1 large egg, at room temperature

1 tablespoon kirsch

⅓ cup (85 grams) heavy cream, whipped to medium-firm peaks

THE CRUST

1 partially baked 9-inch (24-cm) tart shell made from Sweet Tart Dough (page 180)

TO FINISH

8 ounces (250 grams) fresh purple figs (about 4)

Confectioners' sugar for dusting

Coffee Tart / Tarte au Café

Adapted from Pierre Hermé Paris

If you've never had a Pierre Hermé (see page 56) dessert, then I encourage you to make this tart, because it is typically Hermé-esque: its look is simple, its medley of textures is surprising, and its taste—the most important part—is sublime. At the base of the tart is a velvety coffee ganache that, unlike most ganaches, is made with white chocolate. When Pierre and I talked about the dessert, he explained that most tarts of this kind use a bittersweet chocolate ganache to which coffee is added and, "as good as that is, the tarts taste more of chocolate than coffee." In other words, they're mocha. But, as Pierre says, "white chocolate has wonderful texture, makes a good ganache, and carries the coffee flavor without adding much flavor of its own." Pierre covers the cushion of ganache with a layer of featherlight ladyfingers (store-bought ladyfingers are ideal) soaked with another hit of coffee, and then lavishes the top with rosettes of coffee whipped cream. If you're a lily gilder, you can add a shower of milk chocolate shavings.

*   **A word on timing:** Of course the crust can be made ahead, but the coffee cream must be made at least 6 hours, preferably 24 hours, in advance, and the finished tart should be refrigerated for at least 1 hour, all of which makes this the perfect party tart. In fact, the first time I made this tart, I prepared the ganache and finished the dessert (i.e., arranged and soaked the ladyfingers and whipped and piped the cream) while my husband was setting out the glasses and nibbles for apéritifs. Unlikely as it seems, with a little do-ahead work, this elegant tart is a quickie.*

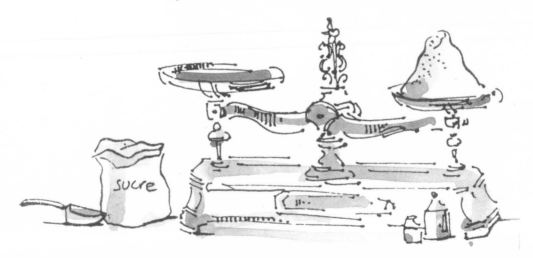

1. **TO MAKE THE COFFEE CREAM**: It's best to do this at least 6 hours ahead or, preferably, the day before you make the tart. Sprinkle the gelatin over the cold water and let it sit for 5 minutes, or until it is soft and spongy, then dissolve it by heating it for 15 seconds in a microwave oven (or do this stovetop); set aside.

2. Line a fine-mesh sieve with a quadruple thickness of damp cheesecloth. Bring the cream to the boil, add the coffee, and stir well, then pour the cream through the sieve; discard the coffee grounds. Wait for 1 minute, then stir the cream— if there's any sediment, strain it again. Stir the sugar and dissolved gelatin into the cream and, once they are incorporated, put the cream into the refrigerator to chill for at least 6 hours, preferably 24.

3. **TO MAKE THE GANACHE**: Line a fine-mesh sieve with a quadruple thickness of damp cheesecloth. Warm the chocolate in a microwave oven (or over a pan of simmering water) just enough to melt it slightly. Pull the chocolate from the heat. Meanwhile, bring the cream to a full boil and stir in the coffee.

4. Pour the cream through the sieve over the white chocolate in two or three additions, stirring gently after each addition with a rubber spatula and only adding more cream when the previous amount is incorporated; discard the coffee grounds. Don't worry if the ganache separates halfway through—it will come together once all the cream is stirred in. Once the ganache is smooth, it should be used immediately.

5. **TO FINISH**: Pour the ganache into the tart shell. Cover the top of the ganache with the ladyfingers, placing the flat of each biscuit against the ganache and arranging the biscuits so that they cover the surface as completely as possible, a job that will require cutting a couple of biscuits to fit into small spaces. Using a pastry brush or a spoon, generously soak the biscuits with the cooled espresso.

6. Working by hand with a whisk, or using a mixer with a whisk attachment, beat the coffee cream until it holds firm peaks. Spoon the cream into a pastry bag fitted with a large star tip and pipe rosettes over the top of the tart, or spoon the cream over the tart and smooth it with a spatula. Refrigerate the tart, away from foods with strong odors, for at least 1 hour to set the ganache. *(The tart can be kept in the refrigerator for up to 8 hours before serving. If the tart has been chilled for a long time, allow it to sit at room temperature for about 30 minutes before serving.)*

7. If you'd like to top the tart with milk chocolate, hold the chocolate over a sheet of parchment or wax paper and, using a vegetable peeler, scrape chocolate shavings onto the paper. Refrigerate the shavings until ready to serve, and scatter them over the tart at the last minute.

THE COFFEE CREAM

1½ teaspoons powdered gelatin

2 tablespoons (30 grams) cold water

2 cups (500 grams) heavy cream

1½ tablespoons (20 grams) sugar

⅓ cup (12 grams) ground-for-espresso coffee, preferably French roast

THE COFFEE GANACHE

10¾ ounces (300 grams) white chocolate, preferably an imported chocolate such as Valrhona Ivoire, finely chopped

1 cup (215 grams) heavy cream

¼ cup (20 grams) ground-for-espresso coffee, preferably French roast

THE CRUST

1 fully baked 9-inch (24-cm) tart shell made with Sweet Tart Dough (page 180)

TO FINISH

10 to 12 store-bought ladyfinger biscuits, split lengthwise

½ cup (125 grams) very strong espresso, cooled

Milk chocolate for shavings (optional)

KEEPING: The crust, coffee cream, and chocolate shavings can be made ahead, and the finished tart can be kept in the refrigerator for up to 8 hours.

AN AMERICAN IN PARIS: Fans of Starbucks' mochaccino might want to serve this tart surrounded by a drizzle of homemade or best-quality store-bought bittersweet chocolate sauce.

Water

Water, water all around, and not a drop to use for tea (or tea tarts), coffee, hot chocolate, sorbet, or anything else in which water is important but meant to go unnoticed. In Paris, the water is very hard, meaning it is full of minerals (and great for your hair—every day is a good hair day in Paris). It also means that when you brew tea in Paris, within two seconds there's an unappealing slick across the top of the cup, and the tea never tastes as good as it does when you have it at one of the city's best tearooms. It is for this reason that many Parisian chefs use mineral water. If the image of a streaky teacup applies to tea at your home, you, too, might want to use a neutral mineral water for all recipes in which water makes a difference. The water used by many Parisian chefs is Volvic. If you can find it, by all means use it; if not, search for a water that is low in sodium and calcium (many supermarket-brand waters fit this bill), and make it your dessert water.

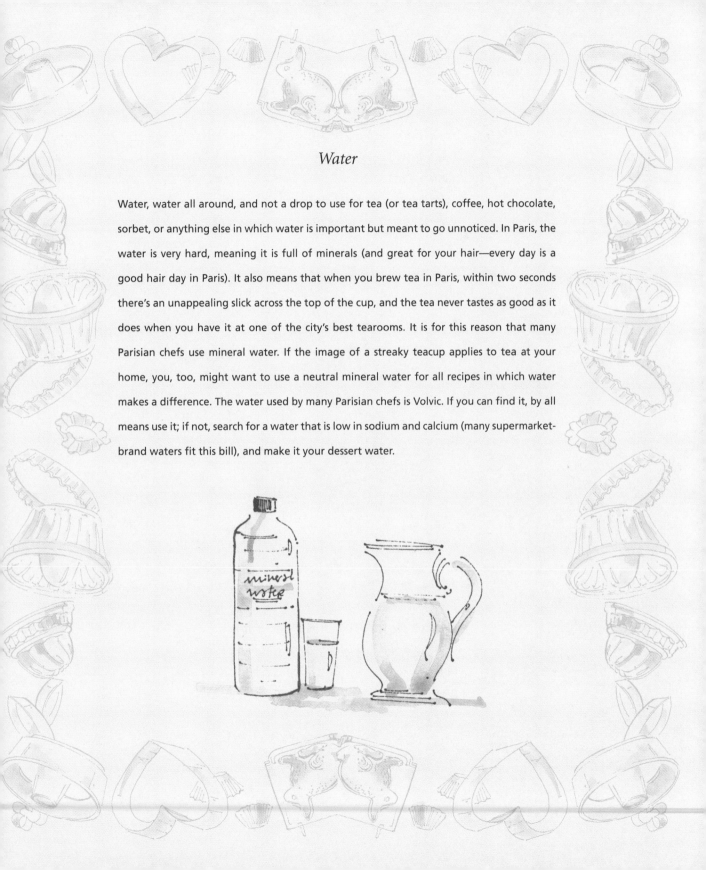

Darjeeling Tea Tart / Tarte au Thé Darjeeling

Adapted from Fauchon

I find it strange but wonderful that tea, an ancient ingredient, is enjoying such a vogue in Parisian pastry. It has found its way into madeleines and financiers, tartes Tatin and crèmes brûlées, ice cream, custards, parfaits, and soufflés too. In this tart from Fauchon, arguably Paris's most famous pâtisserie (see page 128), tea provides the flavor—and a tinge of color—to a filling that can only be called voluptuous. Part sabayon and part custard, it is soft, silken, and deliciously slippery, rich, almost caramel-y, and fully perfumed with the exotic flavor of Darjeeling tea. (If you want to use Fauchon's own Darjeeling, the tea that is used at their pâtisserie, see the Source Guide, page 185.)

If the tart included nothing more than a perfect crust and the pluperfect tea cream, it would be a smash, but there is a finishing touch that guarantees the tart's unforgettability: a crunchy, buttery hazelnut streusel. There have been days when I've had to restrain myself from quadrupling the streusel recipe and making it solo as the ultimate all-indulgent snack. As it is, the recipe makes twice as much as you'll need for this tart, but for reasons of texture (to say nothing of greed), I wouldn't suggest you reduce the proportions.

A word on the crust: *At Fauchon, this tart is made in a hazelnut crust. To do the same, make the Sweet Tart Dough with toasted and skinned ground hazelnuts in place of the almonds.*

1. **TO MAKE THE TEA CREAM:** Bring the water to the boil. Put the tea in a heat-proof bowl, pour the boiling water over it, and allow to steep for 4 minutes, then strain it into a measuring cup; discard the leaves. You'll need ⅔ cup (140 grams) of the tea for the cream.

2. Sprinkle the gelatin over the cold tap water and let it sit for 5 minutes, or until it is soft and spongy, then dissolve it by heating it for 15 seconds in a microwave oven (or do this stovetop); set aside.

3. Bring a saucepan filled with an inch or so of water to a simmer over medium heat. Put the eggs, sugar, and tea in a large metal bowl that can be placed over the pan of water. Off the heat, whisk them together. Set the bowl over the pan, making sure the bottom of the bowl is not touching the simmering water, and cook, whisking constantly, until the cream thickens enough for the whisk to leave slowly dissolving tracks. (This can take between 5 and 10 minutes, depending on the heat you're giving it.) If you have an instant-read thermometer, check the cream—it should be 180°F (80°C). Pull the bowl from the heat and let the cream cool on the counter for about 5 minutes before stirring in the dissolved gelatin. Wait for 5 minutes more, (until the cream is about 114°F [40°C]), then scrape it into a blender (first choice) or food processor.

4. With the machine on high (if you're using a blender), add the butter 4 pieces at a time, then blend or process for 5 minutes (do this in 1-minute spurts if your machine seems to be getting hot), or until the cream is satiny smooth. Pour the cream into the tart shell and chill for at least 3 hours.

5. **TO MAKE THE STREUSEL:** Working in a small bowl with a rubber spatula, beat the butter until smooth. One by one, blend in the remaining ingredients in the order in which they are listed, making sure each ingredient is incorporated before adding the next. Cover the bowl and refrigerate until the mixture is thoroughly cold, about 1 hour.

6. Center a rack in the oven and preheat the oven to 325°F (160°C). Line a baking sheet with parchment paper and keep it close at hand.

7. Using your fingers, break the streusel into pieces of varying sizes. Spread the streusel out on the baking sheet and slide the sheet into the oven. Bake for 10 minutes, then use a metal spatula to break up any large clumps of streusel. Return the streusel to the oven and bake for another 5 minutes or so, until it is golden brown. Cool, still on the pan, to room temperature. *(The streusel can be made up to 2 days ahead and kept in an airtight container at room temperature, or it can be frozen for up to 1 month.)*

THE TEA CREAM

1¼ cups (300 grams) water, preferably a neutral mineral water such as Volvic

2½ tablespoons (15 grams) premium-quality loose Darjeeling tea (see headnote)

¾ teaspoon powdered gelatin

¼ cup (60 grams) cold tap water

4 large eggs

¾ cup (150 grams) sugar

2 sticks (8 ounces; 225 grams) unsalted butter, cut into 16 pieces, at room temperature

1 fully baked 9-inch (24-cm) tart shell made with Sweet Tart Dough (page 180)

THE STREUSEL

3½ tablespoons (1¾ ounces; 50 grams) unsalted butter, at room temperature

6 tablespoons (50 grams) all-purpose flour

½ cup (50 grams) ground skinned hazelnuts

Pinch of salt

¼ cup (50 grams) sugar

¼ cup (25 grams) coarsely chopped skinned hazelnuts

TO FINISH

Confectioners' sugar for dusting (optional)

8. **TO FINISH**: If the pieces of streusel are large, break them up with your fingers, then sprinkle the streusel over the cream, patting it down gently so that it sticks. *(You will have too much streusel for 1 tart. The extra can be nibbled as a snack, sprinkled over ice cream, or frozen.)* If you'd like, give the tart a light dusting of confectioners' sugar before serving.

KEEPING: Although the streusel can be made ahead, this tart is best served the day it is made.

AN AMERICAN IN PARIS: In an act of culinary sacrilege, I sprinkled this streusel over Robert Linxe's already perfect Chocolate Tart (page 62) and found it nothing less than yummy.

LADURÉE Ladurée is so much a part of Paris life that a handful of years ago, when the bakers reworked their recipe for croissants, there were protests from the chic clientele and headlines in the daily newspapers. While this was a problem for Ladurée—one they cleverly solved by keeping both recipes in their repertoire—it was a delight for me. I saw it as another vivid example of how seriously my neighbors in Paris take their food and how deeply they cherish their favorite places.

Even if you've been to Ladurée only once in your life, I think you'll understand why the original shop is held so dear. In part, it has to with the pâtisserie's long history: it was established in 1862 as a boulangerie and became a pastry shop and tea salon in 1871 when a fire forced Ernest Ladurée, its founder, to rebuild. And in part it has to do with its location: it is on the aptly named rue Royale, the imperial street that connects the Place de la Concorde, with its golden Egyptian obelisk and grand fountains, to the Place de la Madeleine, with its classic church and classy boutiques. But mostly it has to do with the shop's interior and the many and marvelous pastries therein.

The instant you enter Ladurée, your eyes are drawn to the ceiling. Even the pyramids of *macarons* (see page 122) and the glossy chocolate creations can't keep you from looking heavenward at the plump cherubs, rosy pink and properly toqued, pulling fat little cakes out of puffy clouds. The frescoes on the ceiling here and in the upstairs dining room date from the turn of the twentieth century and are the work of Chéret, a famous poster artist of the time, who was inspired by the Sistine Chapel and by Garnier's newly built Opera House just a short walk away.

The angelic chefs preside over a room that is always full, no matter the hour. From their cloud-puff perches, they have a daily view of celebrities and tourists, neighborhood habitués and connoisseurs from every corner of Paris, all being served by waitresses in prim black dresses. This scene is repeated on the Champs-Élysées, where a larger, spectacularly decorated Ladurée, complete with a greenhouse dining room modeled after a Gustave Eiffel design, opened in 1997, and in Saint-Germain-des-Prés, where the newest Ladurée patisserie and tea salon was recently tucked into a corner of this artists' corner.

As beautiful as Ladurée is, it endures only in part because of its lavish good looks. It is in largest measure because of its perfect pastry that it remains a *bonne adresse.* Ever since Ernest Ladurée first manned the ovens of his eponymous pâtisserie, Ladurée has had talented pastry chefs leading its kitchen brigades. Today, it is Philippe Andrieu who is responsible for maintaining the classics—the justly famous croissants (both renditions), the rich brioche, the impeccably fashioned tarts, *les grands gâteaux,* and the chocolates—as well as for imagining *les nouvelles créations*—the annual new *macaron,* the Valentine whimsy, the cake that will crown Christmas dinner, and the fall and summer collections that will make fashion news.

That the young Andrieu does this so adroitly is remarkable; that Ladurée has done this for almost a hundred fifty years is astounding, and it's something I think of every time I visit the shop. I also think of how prescient M. Ladurée was to give the pâtisserie his name. *La durée* translates as "the duration," and few other pâtisseries in Paris have gone the duration for as long—or come through it as well—as Ladurée.

Fresh Strawberry and Marshmallow Tart / Tarte aux Fraises à la Guimauve Fraîche

Adapted from Ladurée

Paris's sobriquet should be "City of a Thousand Strawberry Tarts." There isn't a pastry shop that doesn't make one and, happily, most shops make really good ones. In fact, starting in April, when the markets get their first shipment of grown-in-France strawberries and the streets fill with the fruit's strong, sweet, and insistently sensuous scent, it's hard to find a tart that isn't worthy of being bought on the spot and eaten as you make your way to the next pastry shop.

But you'd have to go long and far to find a better strawberry tart than this one created by Philippe Andrieu for Ladurée (see page 96). Its pastry cream is flavored with vanilla and, once cooled, given a lighten-it-up whipping and another measure of butter, technically making it a crème mousseline. Because the second round of butter is added when the cream is cold, the mousseline feels even smoother in your mouth than pastry cream normale. (You'll have more pastry cream than you'll need for this tart, but you shouldn't cut the recipe down—you won't get the satiny smoothness if you do. Instead, tuck the extra cream into the freezer so it will be at the ready for the next time you crave this tart.)

The crème mousseline makes the perfect base for the double-decker strawberry topping, the first deck of which is a thin gloss of barely sweetened crushed berries, the second a series of concentric circles of berries brushed with jelly. Then, interlaced with the berries, is the tart's big surprise: homemade marshmallows flavored with fresh strawberry purée. The marshmallows are sensational, and if you've never made marshmallows at home, you are in for a tremendous treat.

Yes, you can, if you want, skip the marshmallows—the tart will still be extra-special. And you can even dot the tart with store-bought marshmallows, but I hate the thought of your missing the fun of making them for yourself. In fact, the first time I made this tart at home, marshmallows and all, I was so thrilled I took pictures of it and e-mailed them to friends and family too far away to come over for a taste. After I sent the pictures, I realized that, while I had meant to be nice, I had, in fact, been a tease. As one friend said when the picture turned up in her mailbox, "This is unfair—I don't want to see it, I want to eat it!" I pass this lit-tle story along to you so that when you make this tart and are as thrilled as I was, you won't talk about it or show it to anyone who can't get a taste—immediately.

1. **TO MAKE THE PASTRY CREAM**: Bring the milk and vanilla bean (pulp and pod) to a boil in a small saucepan over medium heat. Cover the pan, turn off the heat, and set aside for 10 minutes. Or, if you are using vanilla extract, just bring the milk to a boil and proceed with the recipe, adding the extract before you add the butter to the hot pastry cream.

2. Working in a heavy-bottomed medium saucepan, whisk the yolks, sugar, and cornstarch together until thick and pale. Whisking all the while, very slowly drizzle a quarter of the hot milk onto the yolks. Then, still whisking, pour the rest of the liquid in a steady stream over the tempered yolks. Remove and dis-card the vanilla pod (or save it for another use—see page 29).

3. Put the pan over medium heat and, whisking vigorously and without stop, bring the mixture to the boil. Keep the mixture at the boil, whisking energeti-cally, for 1 to 2 minutes, then remove the pan from the heat and scrape the pastry cream into a clean bowl. Allow the pastry cream to cool on the counter for about 3 minutes.

4. Cut half the butter (5½ tablespoons; 80 grams) into 5 or 6 chunks and stir the chunks into the hot pastry cream, continuing to stir until the butter is melted and incorporated. At this point, the cream needs to be thoroughly chilled. You can either set the bowl into a larger bowl filled with ice cubes and cold water and, to ensure even cooling, stir the cream from time to time, or refrigerate the cream, in which case you should press a piece of plastic wrap against the sur-face to create an airtight seal.

5. When the pastry cream is cold, scrape it into the bowl of a mixer fitted with the whisk attachment. Put the remaining 5½ tablespoons (80 grams) butter in a small bowl and, using a rubber spatula, work the butter until it is soft and creamy. With the mixer on high speed, gradually beat the softened butter into the pastry cream. Keep whipping until the pastry cream is light, smooth, and satiny. The pastry cream can be used now or chilled until needed. *(The cream can be kept tightly covered in the refrigerator for up to 3 days or packed airtight and frozen for 1 month. Defrost overnight in the refrigerator and whip before us-ing to return it to its smooth consistency.)*

THE PASTRY CREAM

1¼ cups (300 grams) whole milk

1 moist, plump vanilla bean, split and scraped (see page 29), or 2 teaspoons pure vanilla extract

3 large egg yolks

½ cup (100 grams) sugar

3 tablespoons (30 grams) cornstarch

1 stick plus 3 tablespoons (9½ ounces; 160 grams) unsalted butter, at room temperature

THE CRUST

1 fully baked 9-inch (24-cm) tart shell made from Sweet Tart Dough (page 180)

TO FINISH

4 cups (1¼ pounds; 600 grams) fresh
    strawberries, hulled

2 teaspoons confectioners' sugar,
    plus more for dusting

Fresh Strawberry Marshmallows
    (page 133) or store-bought
    marshmallows

Red currant jelly

6. **TO ASSEMBLE THE TART:** Fill the tart shell with enough pastry cream to come about ¼ inch (7 mm) from the top of the crust. Smooth (or at least even) the surface of the cream with an offset spatula.

7. Put ¾ cup (115 grams) of the strawberries in a small bowl with the confectioners' sugar and, using a fork, coarsely crush the berries. Allow the berries to sit for 3 minutes, then turn them into a sieve and shake the sieve over the sink several times to get rid of as much liquid as possible. Spoon the crushed berries over the pastry cream, leaving a slim border bare.

8. Cut the remaining berries in half and cut 4 or 5 of the marshmallows (or as many or as few as you'd like) into pieces slightly smaller than the halved strawberries. Now you have a choice: you can either arrange the berries and marshmallows in concentric circles over the top of the tart, alternating the berry halves with the marshmallow pieces, or you can cover the tart with concentric circles of halved berries and then dot the top of the tart with pieces of marshmallow—it will look great either way. For the final touch, warm some red currant jelly on the stovetop or in a microwave oven and, using a pastry feather or brush, paint each strawberry with a little jelly. Serve the tart, or chill it until needed.

KEEPING: The tart should be served cool, and it can be kept in the refrigerator, lightly covered with plastic wrap and away from foods with strong odors, for about 8 hours.

AN AMERICAN IN PARIS: It almost goes without saying that the *crème mousseline* is sensational with raspberries and equally good with blueberries. But it is also a very good base for a tart topped with lightly poached or even roasted apricots, figs, or pineapple or with fresh oranges, mangoes, or even Concord grapes. When I'm using anything other than strawberries or raspberries, I forgo the underlayer of crushed fruit and, regrettably, the marshmallows.

Pastries

and Small Treats for

Occasions Simple or Swell

PÂTISSERIE MULOT

I can't remember when I first went to Pâtisserie Gérard Mulot—could it have been twenty-five years ago?—but I do remember what I bought: a tiny boat-shaped strawberry tartlet. It was about three inches long, the crust cookie-like, the pastry cream speckled with grains of vanilla, and the berries, maybe six *fraises des bois,* brilliantly red, lushly ripe, and vibrantly flavorful. The little treasure was wrapped to go in paper and tied with a ribbon, but I hadn't gone farther than the other side of the street before I'd polished it off in two bites. Then I walked back to the shop, bought another tartlet, and told the woman to forget the ribbon—I knew this one wasn't going far either.

Since then, I've been to Pâtisserie Mulot so many times that I'm certain I could draw the shop on the lively rue de Seine from memory, filling in with accuracy the exact spots for the large rectangles of creamy clafoutis (page 82); the orange tarts topped with diamonds of candied zest; the puffy meringues held together with braids of whipped cream (page 124); the chocolate cakes both round and long, dark and light, sleek and frilly; the clear boxes holding *macarons* (see page 123) in myriad flavors, *tuiles,* and buttery cookies; the long case with the savory offerings, among them my favorite vegetable quiche; the chocolate bonbons; the breads and brownies, brioches, and croissants near the cash register; and, in the front window, given pride of place, the chef's signature fruit tarts and cakes, each topped with a landscape of intricately cut and carefully glazed fruit—and all suitable rivals to a Carmen Miranda headdress.

For all the years I'd been both a fan and a patron, I had never spoken to Gérard Mulot. Of course, I'd seen him: it is a rare day that he is not at the shop, in the kitchen, naturally, but often behind the counters, straightening up the displays, helping customers, packing special orders, or checking supplies, and it is equally rare not to find his wife there as well. As sophisticated as the clientele is and as well known as the shop has become, it is still very much a mom-and-pop business, and elegantly dressed *maman* and *papa* in his white chef's jacket are still attending to every detail. Time after time, I was tempted to just tap the chef on the shoulder to tell him how much pleasure his pastries have brought me over so many years, but I never dared—he always looked too busy and far too intense to be disturbed.

I wish I could tell you that one day, overwhelmed by the deliciousness of his chocolate tart, I marched up to him and planted appreciative kisses on both his cheeks—but I can't. When I finally tapped him on the shoulder, it was because I needed something: recipes for this book. (I knew I couldn't complete the book without nabbing the recipe for his dreamy clafoutis.) Within seconds, I discovered that the chef is just as I'd suspected—busy and intense. But he is also, as I am convinced all the best *pâtissiers* are, open, generous, quick to smile, deeply serious about work, and humble about success. Gérard Mulot was happy to share his recipes and his knowledge, to pass along little *trucs* and shortcuts, and to hear that I had been so loyal for so long. He had only one question: why hadn't I talked to him sooner? I wondered the same thing.

Crème Brûlée

Adapted from Pâtisserie Mulot

Crème brûlée is so popular in America we might almost think we invented it. And, indeed, it's so popular in France the French might even think they invented it. In fact, crème brûlée, a thick baked custard with a crackly broiled sugar topping, is a Spanish invention. Called crema catalana and still referred to by that name in some French cookbooks, it was sometimes made with a sugar topping so thick and hard that the dish was presented with a small hammer, just the tool each diner needed to crack the coating before digging in.

At Gérard Mulot's gleaming white pâtisserie (see page 102), equidistant from l'Église Saint-Sulpice and the regal Sénat, crème brûlée is set out in the display cases ready-to-go. It is made in small foil cups that can be slipped into porcelain molds at home if the crèmes are destined to be dinner party fare, or taken to the nearby Luxembourg Gardens to be eaten en plein air. Enjoyed like this, the custard and the sugar topping are a similar cool temperature. While uniformly cool crème brûlée is a pleasure, a crème brûlée in which the crème is cold and the brûléed sugar is still warm is more dramatic and just that much more interesting. To get this temperature contrast right, you must chill the custard for at least 3 hours before sprinkling it with brown sugar and broiling or blowtorching the topping—the custard needs to be firmly set and very cold to stand up to this blast of heat.

1¼ cups (300 grams) heavy cream

½ cup (120 grams) whole milk

1½ moist, plump vanilla beans, split and scraped (see page 29)

3 large egg yolks

⅓ cup plus 1 tablespoon (75 grams) sugar

About 6 tablespoons sifted brown sugar for topping

1. Center a rack in the oven and preheat the oven to 200°F (90°C). Place six gratin dishes or ramekins on a rimmed baking sheet: the ideal gratins or ramekins for this recipe are round porcelain or glass dishes (although you can, as M. Mulot does, use toss-away aluminum pans) that are just 1 inch (2.5 cm) high and 4 inches (10 cm) across; they should hold about ¾ cup (about 200 ml).

2. Bring the cream, milk, and vanilla beans (pod and pulp) to a boil in a medium saucepan over medium heat. Pull the pan from the heat and set it aside for about 15 minutes (or for up to an hour, if that's more convenient for you).

3. Remove the pods from the cream mixture and discard them or save them for another use (see page 29). Reheat the cream mixture; it should be hot to the touch.

4. Put the yolks and sugar in a medium bowl or, better yet, a 1-quart measuring

cup with a spout and whisk until the yolks are smooth but not airy. Whisking without stop, drizzle in about one-quarter of the hot cream mixture, then add the rest of the liquid in a slow, steady stream. Rap the bowl against the counter to pop the bubbles that will have formed, then pour the custard through a strainer into the dishes, dividing it evenly among them; it will come about two-thirds to three-quarters of the way up the sides.

5. Bake the custards for 50 to 60 minutes, or until the centers are set; if you tap the sides of the dishes, the custards should not shimmy. Transfer the custards to a rack and cool to room temperature.

6. Cover each dish with plastic wrap and chill for at least 3 hours, or for up to 2 days. The custards need to be very cold before they can be brûléed.

7. If you have a blowtorch (Williams-Sonoma sells a small torch just perfect for making crème brûlée), now is the time to use it: just sprinkle the tops of the custards evenly with brown sugar, using about 1 tablespoon for each, then torch away until the sugar bubbles and browns but does not burn. If you're torchless, preheat the broiler and line the bottom of a shallow roasting pan with ice cubes. Sprinkle the tops of the custards with the brown sugar, set the dishes into the ice, and run the custards under the broiler—and don't even think about turning your back on these, let alone answering the phone! As soon as the sugar is bubbly and brown, pull the pan from the broiler. Remove the custards from the ice bath and give them a couple of seconds for the sugar to settle down before serving.

KEEPING: The custard can be made up to 2 days ahead and kept covered in the refrigerator. You can brûlée the sugar and chill the desserts for up to 6 hours, but if you want to have cool custard and a warm topping, serve the dessert as soon as the sugar is brûléed.

AN AMERICAN IN PARIS: The French are not nearly as fond of cinnamon as we are (in fact, most French people will frown at the mere mention of the flavor), but I like the idea of cinnamon-scented crème brûlée and often add a stick or two of cinnamon to the cream mixture before bringing it to the boil, then allow it to infuse for about 20 minutes. (Pick out the cinnamon sticks when you pull out the vanilla beans.) You can use this same technique with slices of fresh ginger, stalks of lemongrass, strips of citrus zest, crushed coffee beans, or a sachet of dried pesticide-free lavender.

Chocolate Mousse / Mousse au Chocolat

Adapted from La Maison du Chocolat

It takes only one spoonful of this chocolate mousse to make it clear why the iconic stature of mousse endures. Of course, there is the taste, the flavor of great chocolate (you have to start with great chocolate—it is an inviolable requirement), smoothed, rounded, softened, and refined by the trinity of cream, butter, and eggs. And there is the texture. In French, mousse means "foam," and it is the foamy texture of mousse, its soft, light, bubbly evanescence, that is its eponymous hallmark. To achieve the proper texture, you should do as La Maison du Chocolat's maître, Robert Linxe (see page 40), told me to do: work gently. Fold the ingredients together with a light touch, and you will be rewarded with a mousse that will live up to its name.

__A word on instant and delayed gratification:__ The sublime texture of La Maison du Chocolat's mousse is very sensitive to time and temperature. It will thicken quickly if left to stand, and it will firm if refrigerated. For these reasons, it is the ideal mousse for people who can make it à la minute, meaning right at the time it should be served. If you want to make the mousse and eat it immediately, use just ¼ cup (65 grams) heavy cream. However, if you want to make the mousse and keep it in the refrigerator for several hours, or even for as long as a day or so, I suggest you increase the quantity of cream to ¾ cup (190 grams). The extra cream will help the mousse maintain its foam.

1. Put the chocolate in a heatproof bowl that is large enough to hold all of the recipe's ingredients and place the bowl over a saucepan containing a small amount of simmering water; the bowl should not touch the water. Heat the chocolate gently, stirring occasionally, until it is melted, then turn off the heat but leave the bowl over the pan.

2. Meanwhile, bring the cream and vanilla bean (pod and pulp) to a boil in a saucepan over medium heat. (Or do this in a microwave oven.)

3. Gently stir the butter into the melted chocolate. When the butter is melted, stir in the heavy cream (discard the vanilla bean or save it for another use; see page 29) and transfer the bowl to the counter. Allow the mixture to cool for 10 minutes, then stir in the 2 egg yolks one at a time.

4. Stir the sugar and cocoa powder together and keep them close at hand. Working in the clean, dry bowl of a mixer with the whisk attachment in place, beat the 5 egg whites with the salt on medium speed until they just start to thicken. When the whites start to form soft peaks, sprinkle in the sugar-cocoa and continue to beat until the whites form firm, glossy peaks. (The little bit of cocoa is included to color the egg whites so they will not appear as streaks in the mousse.)

5. Using a large rubber spatula, stir about one-quarter of the egg whites into the cooled chocolate mixture to lighten it. Delicately fold in the rest of the whites. If you used ¼ cup heavy cream, the mousse is now ready to serve. If you used the larger amount of heavy cream, you will need to chill the mousse for about 30 minutes to set it before serving.

KEEPING: The eat-it-now mousse, made with ¼ cup (65 grams) heavy cream, should be served immediately and should not be refrigerated. (After just a short time in the fridge, the dessert will be more like fudge than mousse.) The save-it-until-later mousse, the one with ¾ cup (190 grams) cream, can be eaten as soon as it sets or kept covered in the refrigerator for a day.

AN AMERICAN IN PARIS: Because I'm a fan of almost everything mocha, I sometimes add ¼ cup (10 grams) crushed coffee beans to the saucepan with the heavy cream and vanilla bean. I bring the cream to the boil, then immediately strain out the beans and discard them.

7 ounces (200 grams) bittersweet chocolate, finely chopped

¼ cup (65 grams) or ¾ cup (190 grams) heavy cream (see head-note)

1 moist, plump vanilla bean, split and scraped (see page 29)

2½ tablespoons (1¼ ounces; 35 grams) unsalted butter, cut into 5 pieces, at room temperature.

2 large eggs, separated, at room temperature

1 tablespoon sugar

1 tablespoon Dutch-processed cocoa powder, sifted

3 large egg whites, at room temperature

Pinch of salt

CHRISTIAN
CONSTANT

$\mathcal{B}$ibliophile that I am, the second I saw Christian Constant's office I knew I'd like him. The room was a riot of papers and books. I could barely see the chocolatier–pastry chef for the towers of books that rose up on his desk and surrounded him. There were more books on the side tables, on the shelves, and even on the chairs. It was all he could do to find a little place for me at the desk, and even as he cleared the books, he opened them, riffled the pages, and drew my attention to things that interested him—and so many things interest Christian Constant.

I wasn't surprised to learn that one of M. Constant's interests is architecture. I had guessed that the first time I went to his shop more than twenty years ago. As much as his office resembles the study of a beloved, disorganized college professor, that's how much his shop, his chocolates, and his desserts resemble the work of a highly disciplined—-but wildly passionate—scientist.

The flagship shop is on the corner of rues d'Assas and de Fleurus, a corner that the chef will always have to share in the history books with Gertrude Stein and Alice B. Toklas, who would have been his neighbors had he come here earlier. Just a few blocks from the Luxembourg Gardens, it is on the ground floor of a typically Parisian apartment building, one with shutters and curlicue grillwork on the windows. But there are no curlicues in Constant's shop. Inside and out, all is gray and white, sleek and cool. The look is spare and sophisticated and it has been M. Constant's trademark for years.

Of course, his most important trademark is his way with all things sweet. His greatest renown has come from his work with chocolate. He was among the first chocolatiers to search out cacao beans and have them roasted and blended to his specifications to create *grands crus,* and he has never stopped experimenting with chocolate. I've got a soft spot for his floral chocolates, ganache-filled squares flavored with a drop of essential oil. The ylang-ylang, rose, and geranium are splendid and unexpected. And I'm fascinated by the chocolates that are made to be eaten while smoking a cigar! Working with a chemist's care, M. Constant isolated the flavors in a cigar, broke down the point at which these flavors appear as the cigar is being smoked, and created chocolates to eat at each stage. These chocolates, as well as his work with the French Institute of Taste to develop a vocabulary for chocolate, are facets of the same restless curiosity that has created, among many other irresistibles, a light chocolate mousse accented with green jasmine tea, a mille-feuille with pears, and a dark-as-midnight cake that blends chocolate and candied lemon.

Constant's boutique is small, but his offerings are varied and of the kind that quickly end up on your favorites list. No matter the season, I have to have one of his superb ice creams or sorbets. And his chocolate cakes (see page 38 for one example) and puddings (see page 110) are as special as you would hope they would be. Ditto for his cookies and each of his several chocolate tarts, especially the chocolate and banana tart he created for the chocolate-adoring designer Sonia Rykiel (page 66). And then there are the less perishable offerings—the books. Not those in his office, but the ones for sale in the shop, most of which he has written, some of which are scholarly, others of which are cookery, and all of which further explore his delicious obsession: chocolate.

Chocolate Bread Pudding /

Pudding au Chocolat

Adapted from Christian Constant

Christian Constant (see page 108) is one of Paris's most creative chocolatiers, but after tasting this dessert, I decided he must be one of the city's most modest as well. Modesty is the only way to explain his having named this lavish dessert pudding au chocolat. *He didn't even bother to mention the bread part of the pudding—no small thing when the bread is golden brioche or challah. This is a very easy-to-make bread pudding that would be at home at any grand restaurant. It is studded with candied fruit and piquant stem ginger, rich with eggs, and luxuriant with chocolate. It emerges from the oven proudly puffed, covered with a light sugar crackle, and is as irresistibly seductive as a siren's song. Yes, it is pudding, but of the deluxe persuasion.*

A word on stem ginger: These are whole knobs of ginger that have been candied and thoroughly saturated with sugar syrup. You can find jars of stem ginger in syrup in the specialty fruit or baking section of supermarkets, and you can find Chinese stem ginger in pottery crocks in Asian markets.

1. Center a rack in the oven and preheat the oven to 325°F (160°C). Butter a 13 x 9 x 2-inch (32.5 x 24 x 5-cm) Pyrex or porcelain baking dish, dust the interior with sugar, and tap out the excess. Place on a baking sheet and set aside.

2. The candied fruit, stem ginger, and stale bread all need to be cut into pieces. It's best to coarsely chop the candied fruit (if you've got candied cherries, though, you might want to leave them whole), finely chop the ginger (it's got some heat and bite, and you wouldn't want to get too much of it at one time), and tear the bread into pieces about 2 inches (5 cm) on a side. Put the fruit and bread in the baking pan and toss them together with your hands.

3. Bring the milk, the 2¼ cups (450 grams) sugar, and the vanilla bean (pod and pulp) to the boil in a large saucepan, stirring occasionally. Meanwhile, put the eggs and yolks in a mixing bowl and whisk them for a minute or two, just to blend.

4. When the milk is boiling and the sugar has dissolved, pull the pan from the heat and remove the vanilla bean; discard the bean or save it for another use (see page 29). Whisking the eggs all the while, slowly pour the hot milk into the mixing bowl. Switch to a rubber spatula and stir in the chopped chocolate, stirring gently until it is melted. Strain the chocolate custard over the bread and fruit.

5. Slide the baking sheet setup into the oven and bake the pudding for 30 to 35 minutes, or until a knife inserted into the center comes out clean. Transfer the pudding to a cooling rack and let it rest until it is just warm or at room temperature—both nice temperatures for serving.

KEEPING: The pudding is great warm or at room temperature and served the day it is made, but few people turn down pudding that's been covered, refrigerated for up to 1 day, and brought back to room temperature.

AN AMERICAN IN PARIS: I love this pudding with plump dried fruit in place of the candied fruit and stem ginger. Sometimes I make the pudding with pitted prunes, sometimes with dried cherries, and sometimes with sweet dried apricots. To be on the safe side, I usually plump the fruit before I toss it with the bread. To plump fruit that looks a little dry, you can either steam it for a minute or two or dunk it into a pan of simmering water for 30 to 60 seconds, drain, and pat dry. This little bit of rehydration is an insurance policy guaranteeing that hard fruit (which won't soften when it's baked) won't spoil your great dessert.

2¼ cups (450 grams) sugar, plus more for dusting the pan

10 ounces (280 grams) assorted high-quality candied fruit, such as glacéed cherries, orange peel, pineapple pieces, and/or angelica

3 knobs stem ginger in syrup (see headnote), drained and patted dry

9 ounces (250 grams) stale bread, preferably brioche, challah, or other egg bread

3 cups (750 grams) whole milk

1 moist, plump vanilla bean, split and scraped (see page 29)

5 large eggs, at room temperature

8 large egg yolks, at room temperature

9 ounces (250 grams) bittersweet chocolate, finely chopped

Ali-Babas

Adapted from Pâtisserie Stohrer

While most of us are familiar with baba au rhum, *a little yeast-raised puff-topped cake soaked to dripping with rum, and with savarin, the same cake and the same soak but ring-shaped with a whipped cream center, these popular desserts are* nouveaux *compared to the original, the Ali-Baba, created in the early eighteenth century by Nicolas Stohrer for his patron, Stanislas Leszczynski, the exiled king of Poland.*

In its first incarnation, the Ali-Baba, named for the hero of 1001 Tales of the Arabian Nights, *was flavored and colored by an infusion of saffron and heavy Malaga wine or, in a pinch, Madeira. Grapes, raisins, angelica, and candied lemons were kneaded into the dough and the Ali-Baba was baked to a deep purplish tint. Right before serving, the cake was given a thorough drenching in a sweet saffron and Malaga syrup.*

Had Pâtisserie Stohrer, the oldest pastry shop in Paris (see page 150), insisted on remaining faithful to its founder's recipe, it is unlikely this cake would have survived into the twenty-first century. But those who followed Nicolas Stohrer kept the Ali-Baba alive by revising the recipe regularly to meet each generation's changing tastes. Today's Ali-Baba is still a close-grained yeast-raised cake, but gone are the saffron and wine, grapes, and candied fruits. These days, the yeasted cake is dunked in a rum syrup, then its top cap is sliced off, the cake is given a layer of pastry cream and rum-flamed raisins, and the top is replaced. The baba is appropriately boozy and inordinately good.

A word on pans and mixers: The baba au rhum *and* savarin *are made with the same dough used to make an Ali-Baba, but the traditional pan for individual* babas au rhum *is a short, cylindrical metal mold with slightly flared sides, and the traditional pan for a savarin is a ring mold. You can use either to make these Ali-Babas, or you can do as I do: use a regular-sized muffin pan in which the molds are about 2¾ inches (6.5 cm) across and have a capacity of ⅓ to ½ cup (80 to 125 grams). (Measure the capacity by pouring water into the molds.) As for the mixer, the most efficient way to beat the baba dough is with a heavy-duty stand mixer, since it needs to be beaten for about 10 minutes.*

1. **TO MAKE THE DOUGH:** Generously butter a 12-mold muffin tin (see above) and set it aside.
2. Stir the water, yeast, and sugar together in the bowl of a heavy-duty stand mixer. When the yeast is dissolved, add the flour and salt. Fit the mixer with the dough hook and beat on medium speed until the ingredients form a moist ball, about 2 minutes. Switch to the paddle attachment, add 2 of the eggs, and beat on medium-low speed for 3 minutes. Add the remaining 2 eggs and, when the eggs are incorporated, increase the mixer speed to medium-high and beat for 3 minutes. Add the cooled butter and beat for 5 more minutes, still on medium-high speed. At this point the dough should be fairly thin (more like a batter) and as smooth and creamy as a hollandaise sauce.
3. Divide the dough evenly among the muffin molds; each mold will be about half-full. Put a piece of parchment or wax paper over the pan, set it aside in a warm place, and allow the dough to rise for 25 to 30 minutes, or until it fills the molds to about the three-quarters mark.
4. While the dough is rising, center a rack in the oven and preheat the oven to 350°F (180°C).
5. Remove the paper, put the muffin tin on a baking sheet, and slide the baking sheet into the oven. As you close the oven door, slip the handle of a wooden spoon into it to keep it slightly ajar. Bake the babas for 25 to 28 minutes, or until golden brown. Transfer the pan to a cooling rack and let the babas sit for 5 minutes before unmolding them onto the rack to cool to room temperature. *(The babas can be kept in a covered container for 1 day at room temperature or wrapped airtight and frozen for up to 1 month; defrost and bring to room temperature before soaking.)*

THE DOUGH

⅓ cup (80 grams) water, at warm
 room temperature
1 packet (2¼ teaspoons; 7 grams)
 active dry yeast
3 tablespoons (40 grams) sugar
1 cup (140 grams) all-purpose flour
¼ teaspoon salt
4 large eggs, at room temperature
6 tablespoons (3 ounces; 90 grams)
 unsalted butter, melted and
 cooled

THE SYRUP

1¼ cups (300 grams) water

¾ cup (150 grams) sugar

¼ cup (60 grams) dark rum

THE CREAM

⅓ cup (50 grams) moist, plump
  raisins

2 tablespoons (20 grams) dark rum

1 cup (400 grams) Vanilla Pastry
  Cream (page 179), chilled

6. **TO MAKE THE SYRUP:** Bring the water and sugar just to the boil in a small saucepan. Pour the syrup into a deep bowl and allow it to cool for 15 minutes, then pour in the rum. *(The syrup can be covered and refrigerated for up to 1 week.)*

7. **TO MAKE THE CREAM:** Soak the raisins in hot water for about 4 minutes, until they are puffed. Drain, drop them into a small saucepan, and, stirring constantly, warm them over low heat. When the raisins are very hot, pull the pan from the heat, pour the rum over them, and, standing back, ignite the rum with a match. Swirl the pan until the flames go out. Cool the raisins to room temperature, then stir them into the chilled pastry cream. *(The cream can be kept tightly covered in the refrigerator for up to 3 days.)*

8. **TO SOAK THE BABAS:** Find a pan that is large enough to hold the babas and keep it nearby on the counter (I use a shallow roasting pan). To help the babas take in as much syrup as possible, use a small paring knife to poke about six slits in each cake. As you poke each baba, drop it into the bowl with the rum syrup and turn it around in the syrup for a minute or so. This isn't a job to do by halves—the babas should be drenched. Carefully, using a large serving spoon, lift the cakes out of the syrup and place in the pan. If there is any syrup left over, spoon or pour it over the babas. Cover the pan lightly with wax paper and transfer it to the refrigerator. The babas should be thoroughly chilled before you fill them with cream. *(If you need to keep the babas in the refrigerator for more than 3 hours, cover the pan tightly; do not keep the cakes refrigerated for longer than 1 day.)*

9. **TO FINISH THE BABAS:** When the babas are cold, use a thin sharp knife to slice off the top third or so of each one. (If you made the babas in baba molds, they may be topped by a crown; if so, slice off the crown.) Top each baba with a spoonful of pastry cream—you should have just enough to go around—and cover the cream with the baba's top piece. Serve now, or wrap well and refrigerate for up to 6 hours.

KEEPING: The babas, their soaking syrup, and the cream can all be made a few days ahead. Even the filled babas can be prepared up to 6 hours ahead, making these easy fare for entertaining.

AN AMERICAN IN PARIS: Since the pastry chefs at Stohrer have played around with this recipe, I feel completely comfortable playing my own variations on this classic. While I'm a sucker for the rum-raisin pastry cream, I sometimes fill the babas with Robert Linxe's Chocolate Mousse (page 106) or slice unfilled babas and serve them alongside the mousse. Unfilled, the babas become traditional *babas au rhum*; if you fill the babas with lightly sweetened whipped cream, another luscious variation, you end up with a *baba chantilly*.

BOULANGERIE KAYSER

Sometimes when I'm waiting in line at Eric Kayser's bakery (where there's always a line), I wonder what Kayser's great-grandfather, the first of four generations of millers and bakers in the family, would make of his offspring's success. Today, at thirty-seven, Eric Kayser has the eager look of a mischievous boy, but he is the director of an empire of bread and pastry shops and a mentor to bakers around the world. In fact, I initially heard about Eric Kayser in 1995 from Nancy Silverton, the celebrated founder of La Brea Bakery in Los Angeles, who urged me to taste Kayser's baguette—the baguette that has since become my favorite in Paris.

When I first lined up for the baguette, Eric Kayser had only one bakery in the lively fifth *arrondissement,* the shop at 8 rue Monge. It was, as it still is, half a block from the rollicking weekly market at Maubert-Mutualité and in the center of a neighborhood chockablock with shops selling everything you could ever imagine putting on a baguette, from perfectly aged cheeses and vine-ripened tomatoes to Greek olives, Scandinavian herring, and Middle Eastern hummus.

Today there are several other Kayser bakeries in Paris (see page 187), including one in a historically classified building just a few doors down from the original shop. On offer there are cakes, breads, and prepared foods made strictly from organic, or *biologique,* products. There are also bakeries in Japan and Israel.

Without question, Eric Kayser is best known as a *boulanger* and most admired for the way he uses modern techniques and technology to produce breads with flavors and textures his great-grandfather would recognize and love. But since the day he opened his first bakery, M. Kayser, like bread bakers of old, has sold some simple cakes, cookies, and tarts, and with these he has proved he has a special feel for sweets.

I'm sure there are now scores of people who make a special trip to Boulangerie Kayser for the sweets alone. If they're like me, they fall for the baker's *brioche au sucre,* rounds of brioche dough pricked with a knife point to contain their normal exuberant puffing and covered with sugar crystals or, in the deluxe version, a little crème fraîche custard. Or maybe they share my weakness for anything Eric Kayser does with apples. One day, unable to decide which apple dessert I wanted quickly enough to keep the line at the counter moving, I bought every apple dessert he had: I bought a *tarte Normande,* an apple and custard tart; a *tarte aux pommes et aux amandes,* a pile-up of baked apples and sliced almonds that reminds me of my grandmother's apple cake, the one I can't reproduce; and half-a-dozen *Fondants aux Pommes* (page 120), cupcake-type sweets that have barely enough batter to hold their apples and raisins in place. M. Kayser's simple fruit tarts are lovely, his pound cakes flawless, his almond and chocolate chip *Tigrés* (page 118) addictively scrumptious, and his brownies good enough to make you think he might be part American.

While America would be proud to claim him as her own, one taste of his baguette, his tarts, or his tender almond croissants proclaims him a son of the *Bleu, Blanc, Rouge.* But with Eric Kayser's entrepreneurial spirit showing no signs of flagging, who knows? There could be a Boulangerie Kayser in our future.

Tiger Tea Cakes / Tigrés

Adapted from Maison Kayser

The only thing that's the least bit tigerish about these irresistible butter-and-almond tea cakes is their light chocolate striping, a result of folding chopped chocolate (or mini chocolate chips) into the batter just before popping the little cakes into the oven. Tigrés, a Parisian creation, are very simple cakes, sometimes topped with a squiggle of chocolate ganache and sometimes not. Although you can find them all over their native city, I love the tiger cakes at Eric Kayser's bustling bread shop (see page 116) for just one reason: they're perfect. They are rich and buttery, of course, but they are also beautifully moist and tightly crumbed, like a great pound cake. Kayser makes his tigrés in 2½-inch (6-cm) dome-shaped molds, so that the finished cakes line up on the counter like so many igloos, but muffin tins, mini or regular, work like a charm.

1. Working in a medium mixing bowl with a whisk, beat the egg whites just to break them up. Add the ground almonds, sugar, flour, and corn syrup and stir until the batter is smooth. Cover the bowl tightly with plastic wrap and refrigerate for at least 2 hours, or as long as overnight.

2. When you are ready to make the *tigrés,* position the racks to divide the oven into thirds and preheat the oven to 350°F (180°C). Butter enough muffin molds to make 16 large *tigrés:* if you have muffin pans with molds that hold about ⅓ cup (85 grams), you should be able to make 16 cakes; if you are using mini-muffin molds with a 2-tablespoon capacity, you should be able to make 48 cakes. Remove the batter from the refrigerator.

3. Put the butter in a small saucepan and bring it to the boil over medium heat. Remove the butter from the heat and stir it into the batter. When the batter is no longer warm, stir in the chocolate.

4. Spoon about 3 tablespoons batter into each buttered regular muffin mold or 1 tablespoon into each mini-muffin mold. Bake the cakes for 15 to 20 minutes, or until they are puffed and golden; a knife inserted in the center should come out clean. Allow the cakes to cool for 2 to 3 minutes, then turn them out onto racks to cool to room temperature.

5. When the cakes are cool, you can top them with ganache, if you wish. To come as close as possible to Eric Kayser's dome-shaped *tigrés,* turn your cakes upside down. Spoon the ganache into a small pastry bag fitted with a star tip and pipe a small rosette of ganache in the center of each *tigré.*

KEEPING: *Tigrés* will keep in a covered container at room temperature for up to 3 days (although ganache-topped *tigrés* are best beaten the day they are made). Packed airtight, the cakes can be frozen for up to 1 month.

AN AMERICAN IN PARIS: I like to go over the top with these, treating each little tea cake like a baby birthday cake. I cut the muffin-sized cakes horizontally into two layers and fill them with ganache, then cover them with chocolate glaze (page 148)—and if I'm feeling extravagant, I top each with a rosette of whipped cream.

6 large egg whites, at room temperature

2¼ cups (235 grams) ground blanched almonds

¾ cup (150 grams) sugar

⅓ cup (45 grams) all-purpose flour

1½ tablespoons (25 grams) light corn syrup

1 stick plus 7 tablespoons (7½ ounces; 210 grams) unsalted butter

5 ounces (145 grams) bittersweet chocolate, finely chopped, or mini chips

Bittersweet chocolate ganache (page 66, Step 1) (optional)

Soft Apple Cakes / Fondants aux Pommes

Adapted from Maison Kayser

Although these look like muffins, they are really small snack cakes. They are thick with sweet apples and rum-soaked raisins suspended in soft, creamy cake. At Boulangerie Kayser (see page 116), these are baked in the French equivalent of cupcake pans, individual narrow cylinders of classically patterned brown baking paper, taller and slimmer than the molds in standard American muffin tins, but similar in spirit. They are sold from trays on the counter, often to youngsters hungry for an after-school treat and just as often to grown-ups longing for something sweet, simple, satisfying, and easy to eat out of hand.

These bake perfectly in standard muffin tins, the ones in which the molds are about 2¾ inches (6.5 cm) in diameter, but you must use cupcake liners to keep them from sticking.

½ cup (60 grams) moist, plump
    raisins

2 tablespoons (30 grams) dark rum

Juice of ½ lemon

3 to 4 large apples, such as Fuji, Gala,
    or Golden Delicious, peeled and
    cored

¾ cup (105 grams) all-purpose flour

½ teaspoon double-acting baking
    powder

Pinch of salt

3 large eggs, preferably at room
    temperature

½ cup (100 grams) sugar

1½ teaspoons pure vanilla extract

4 tablespoons (2 ounces; 60 grams)
    unsalted butter, melted and
    cooled

1. Soak the raisins in hot water for about 4 minutes, until they are puffed. Drain, drop them into a small saucepan, and, stirring constantly, warm them over low heat until they are very hot. Remove the pan from the heat, pour the rum over the raisins, and, standing back, ignite the rum with a match. Swirl the pan until the flame goes out. (*You can use the raisins as soon as they cool or cover them and keep them overnight.*)

2. Position the racks to divide the oven into thirds and preheat the oven to 325°F (160°C). Line 20 muffin molds with cupcake liners.

3. Put the lemon juice in a large bowl. Cut each apple in half from top to bottom, cut each half into ¼-inch (7-mm) slices, and then cut the slices crosswise in half. Toss the slices in the bowl with the lemon juice.

4. Whisk together the flour, baking powder, and salt.

5. Put the eggs and sugar in a mixer fitted with the whisk attachment and beat on medium-high speed until the eggs are pale and voluminous, about 4 minutes. Beat in the vanilla. Switch to a large rubber spatula and stir a couple of spoonfuls of the batter into the melted butter. Working gently, fold the flour into the remaining batter, followed by the melted butter, apples, and raisins.

6. Spoon the batter into the lined muffin tins, filling each mold just about to the top, and slip the tins into the oven. Bake for 25 to 28 minutes, rotating the tins

top to bottom and front to back halfway through the baking; the cakes are done when a knife inserted in the center comes out clean. Transfer the tins to a rack and wait for 5 minutes before gently lifting the cakes, in their papers, from them. Allow the cakes to cool to tepid or room temperature before serving.

KEEPING: Tucked back into the muffin tins and covered with plastic wrap, the small cakes will keep for a day at room temperature.

AN AMERICAN IN PARIS: I've found that this recipe works perfectly as a cake. Butter an 8-inch (20-cm) springform pan, line the bottom with parchment paper, and set the pan on a baking sheet. Fill the pan with the batter, and bake for 70 to 80 minutes, or until a knife inserted in the center of the cake comes out clean. Transfer the pan to a cooling rack and cool the cake for 10 minutes before carefully running a blunt knife between the cake and the sides of the pan and removing the ring of the springform. Leave the cake on the pan's base and cool to tepid or room temperature. Serve with gobs of lightly sweetened whipped cream.

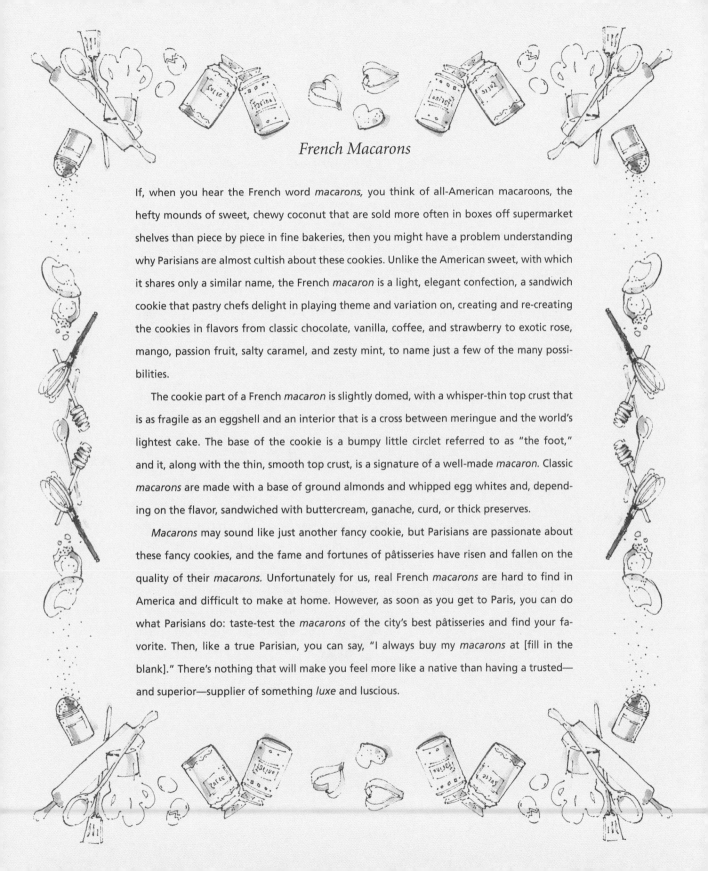

French Macarons

If, when you hear the French word *macarons,* you think of all-American macaroons, the hefty mounds of sweet, chewy coconut that are sold more often in boxes off supermarket shelves than piece by piece in fine bakeries, then you might have a problem understanding why Parisians are almost cultish about these cookies. Unlike the American sweet, with which it shares only a similar name, the French *macaron* is a light, elegant confection, a sandwich cookie that pastry chefs delight in playing theme and variation on, creating and re-creating the cookies in flavors from classic chocolate, vanilla, coffee, and strawberry to exotic rose, mango, passion fruit, salty caramel, and zesty mint, to name just a few of the many possibilities.

The cookie part of a French *macaron* is slightly domed, with a whisper-thin top crust that is as fragile as an eggshell and an interior that is a cross between meringue and the world's lightest cake. The base of the cookie is a bumpy little circlet referred to as "the foot," and it, along with the thin, smooth top crust, is a signature of a well-made *macaron.* Classic *macarons* are made with a base of ground almonds and whipped egg whites and, depending on the flavor, sandwiched with buttercream, ganache, curd, or thick preserves.

Macarons may sound like just another fancy cookie, but Parisians are passionate about these fancy cookies, and the fame and fortunes of pâtisseries have risen and fallen on the quality of their *macarons.* Unfortunately for us, real French *macarons* are hard to find in America and difficult to make at home. However, as soon as you get to Paris, you can do what Parisians do: taste-test the *macarons* of the city's best pâtisseries and find your favorite. Then, like a true Parisian, you can say, "I always buy my *macarons* at [fill in the blank]." There's nothing that will make you feel more like a native than having a trusted—and superior—supplier of something *luxe* and luscious.

Whipped Cream—Filled Meringues /

Meringues Chantilly

Adapted from Pâtisserie Mulot

Meringue is one of the most magical mixtures in the pastry repertory. It is nothing more than egg whites and sugar, but it is a testament to the pastry chef's imagination and craft that these two basic ingredients can become something so wondrous. Even the simplest meringues, big puffs or frilly rosettes, the kind you see stacked in every pâtisserie, have an eye-catching whimsicality and an almost universal appeal. Pipe the meringues with care, bake them until their outsides are just lightly caramelized and their insides an almost impossible combination of crisp and chewy, sandwich two of the small treats together with perfectly whipped cream, what the French call chantilly, and you have delicious proof that the sum is greater than its parts.

You can find meringues chantilly at most pastry shops in Paris, but nowhere can you find a better one than this. Nor, for that matter, will you find a pâtissier with more affection for this classic than Gérard Mulot (see page 102), a pastry chef who understands the sweet's beauty, simplicity, and deliciousness. As he was giving me the recipe, M. Mulot fussed with the details. "Try to pipe the whipped cream between the meringues in an attractive pattern," he urged, explaining that he likes to pipe a somewhat twisted line. "And don't forget that you can top the cream with a few berries. Thin pieces of strawberries are really nice with this," he added. As he reread his handwritten instructions and gave me last-minute advice, no one would ever have guessed that this was a pastry Gérard Mulot has made just about every day of his life for more than thirty years. It was clear that for him, the little sweet hadn't lost a whit of its charm.

1. **TO MAKE THE MERINGUES**: Center a rack in the oven and preheat the oven to 250°F (120°C). Line a baking sheet with parchment paper, and fit a large pastry bag with a plain ½-inch (1.5-cm) piping tip; keep these close at hand.

2. Put the egg whites in a clean, dry mixer bowl, fit the mixer with the whisk attachment, and start to beat the whites at medium-low speed. When the whites turn opaque and start to thicken, increase the mixer speed to high—but don't walk away. When you see that the whites are forming peaks, add the granulated sugar in a stream, then continue to whip until the whites form firm, glossy peaks. Switch to a rubber spatula and gently and gradually fold in the confectioners' sugar. (You might find it helpful to add the sugar through a sieve.) Work quickly and delicately so that you deflate the batter as little as possible. The meringue is now ready and should be used immediately.

3. Spoon the meringue into the pastry bag and pipe out about 12 plump mounds (part oval, part lozenge), each about 3 inches long by 2 inches wide by about ½ inch high (7.5 x 5 x 1.5 cm), on the prepared baking sheet. Dust the meringues with confectioners' sugar (a sieve or a sugar duster does the job best) and let them sit on the counter for about 10 minutes so that the sugar can pearl, or form little beads.

4. Slide the baking sheet into the oven, slip the handle of a wooden spoon into the oven to keep the door slightly ajar, and bake the meringues for 2 hours, until they are firm, dry, and very lightly caramel colored. Turn off the heat, close the oven door, and allow the meringues to dry in the oven for 4 hours or for as long as overnight. Transfer the meringues, parchment and all, to racks to cool to room temperature.

5. When they are cool, run a metal spatula under the meringues to loosen them from the paper. *(The meringues can be made up to 5 days ahead and kept covered, cool, and, above all, dry.)*

6. **TO MAKE THE CHANTILLY**: Fit a large pastry bag with a ½-inch (1.25-cm) open star tip and keep it close at hand. Line a baking sheet with parchment paper. If you have the time, pop your mixer bowl into the freezer for 30 minutes or so.

7. Pour the cream and vanilla extract into the mixer bowl, fit the mixer with the whisk attachment, and, working at medium speed, begin to whip the cream. When the cream starts to form soft peaks, gradually add the confectioners' sugar. Increase the mixer speed to high and whip the cream until it holds firm but supple peaks.

8. **TO FINISH**: Spoon the cream into the pastry bag and pipe a pretty twist of cream onto the flat of one meringue. Sandwich the cream with the flat of a sec-

THE MERINGUES

3 large egg whites, at room temperature

½ cup (100 grams) sugar

1 cup (100 grams) confectioners' sugar, sifted, plus more for dusting

THE *CHANTILLY*

2 cups (500 grams) chilled heavy cream

1 teaspoon pure vanilla extract

½ cup (50 grams) confectioners' sugar, sifted

Sliced strawberries or chocolate shavings for topping (optional)

ond meringue, and place the sandwich on the parchment-lined baking sheet, balancing it on one of the long, thin sides of the meringues. Pipe another decorative twist of cream down the center of the sandwich so that it mounds above the meringues. Continue with the rest of the batch. If you like, you can top the meringues with cut strawberries or chocolate shavings. Chill until needed.

KEEPING: The meringues can be made ahead and stored, covered, in a cool, dry place for up to 5 days, and the *chantilly* can be whipped up to 2 hours ahead and kept covered in the refrigerator. (If necessary, whisk it by hand to bring back its consistency before piping.) Once assembled, the *meringues chantilly* can be kept loosely covered in the refrigerator for about 6 hours. Certainly, they should be eaten the day they are made.

AN AMERICAN IN PARIS: I have brought *joie* to the dinner table by sandwiching the meringue puffs with ice cream. The best thing to do is to construct the ice cream sandwiches, put them on a parchment-lined baking sheet, and slide the sheet into the freezer. Once the sandwiches are frozen, wrap each one individually in a double thickness of plastic wrap. Protected from everything but snackers, the sandwiches can stay in the freezer for up to 1 week. These sandwiches are great unadorned, but they're sensational topped with either whipped cream or hot fudge sauce or a little (or a lot) of both.

Eggs

Eggs are often called one of nature's most perfect foods, but as an American baker working to recreate Paris pastries in a New York City kitchen, I've come to think of eggs as nature's most accommodating food and of French chickens as nature's most thoughtful creatures—after all, they are considerate enough to lay eggs that are exactly the same size as American eggs.

All of the recipes in this book were tested with American eggs graded "large," eggs that happily—and accurately—match any Paris pastry chef's egg size of choice, *moyenne.* Having an exact match is not so serious when a recipe calls for just one egg. But as the number of eggs mounts, so can the errors if you use anything but large eggs.

It goes without saying that using the best-quality eggs and keeping them in the best condition will give you the best desserts. These days, I buy organic eggs (called *biologique,* or *bio* for short, in France) or, if they are not available, eggs from hormone- and antibiotic-free chickens fed vegetarian diets. If you are not accustomed to cooking with these eggs, do a little comparison test for yourself—you'll find they have yolks that are more deeply colored than those of supermarket-brand eggs (they make a gorgeous pastry cream) and a flavor that is fuller. Indeed, if all you've ever eaten is supermarket eggs, you may be surprised to find that eggs actually have flavor.

Eggs of any kind should be kept refrigerated until needed. If a recipe calls for separated eggs, separate the eggs while they are cold (chilled eggs separate more easily than warm eggs), and whip the whites when they come to room temperature (warm whites whip to a fuller volume). It is almost always a good idea to work with eggs that are at room temperature. In fact, for most recipes, all of the ingredients should be at the same temperature so that none of the ingredients are shocked by cold and none, like butter, are hardened by the addition of something straight from the chilly fridge.

FAUCHON   I've always thought that a first visit to Paris should include the basics: the Louvre, the Eiffel Tower, the Impressionist collection at the Musée d'Orsay, Nôtre-Dame, the Sainte-Chapelle, a walk down the Champs-Élysées, an espresso at a grand café, and a leisurely ogle at Fauchon. For many people, Fauchon is to food what the Louvre is to art: the best place to get an overview of the field. And it has been this way for more than a hundred years, ever since Auguste Fauchon pushed his fruit carts into the Place de la Madeleine.

For sure, the Place de la Madeleine wasn't then what it is today—the site of a grand church surrounded by a flower market, a last-minute ticket booth for concerts and plays, elegant clothiers, and chic restaurants and food emporia, the chic-est among them Fauchon, which now covers an entire corner of the impressive square. But, by 1886, the Place de la Madeleine was already showing signs of what it would become, and M. Fauchon opened two boutiques, which were soon followed by others, each showcasing another aspect of gastronomy, so that soon wines, teas, coffees, cakes, pastries, breads, and luxury groceries were added to the fruit. Then, as now, everything was displayed as beautifully as in a Fantin-Latour still life.

I've been a Fauchon ogler and shopper since my first trip to Paris thirty years ago, when I remember turning the corner into the Place de la Madeleine and coming upon the chocolate-brown awnings that shaded a huge window of exotic fruits laid out in an array so stunning they inspired sketchers and photographers. One store down was the prepared foods market, and across the street, the pastry shop with fanciful cakes that seemed to have been created by sugar-plum fairies.

Today the fruit boutique is a tea salon, the prepared foods boutique has been redesigned, and there is a grander grocery store with more than a hundred varieties of tea, as many jams and jellies, forty kinds of chocolate, and, of course, exotic fruits and vegetables. The wine cellar, with 2,500 different bottles, has been revamped. And the awnings are now ballerina pink.

What seems not to have changed is the pâtisserie. Over the years, Fauchon has had a singular knack for hiring some of France's most talented pastry chefs, and each has added his creations to the house's repertoire. Of course, there are the classics: the éclairs (page 130) and the myriad other sweets that are made from cream puff dough, including *les religieuses,* roly-poly puffs filled with pastry cream and circled with whipped cream to recall a cleric's stiff collar; the mille-feuilles; the *dacquoise* with hunks of hazelnuts; and the parade of croissants, brioches, and *pains aux raisins* that makes each morning a celebration. But there are also *les nouveautés,* the new additions that have made their way into the pantheon of classics. While everyone has his or her favorites—and you will too, even after one visit—I'm partial to the lemon tart, with a filling that goes satin one better in the smooth department; the tea tart (page 92), created when the new *salon de thé* was opened and flavored so deftly that it captures the mystery of Darjeeling; and the Auguste, five small chocolate cakes that, when pieced together, form an intricate puzzle.

Now that I think about it, maybe a visit to Fauchon is even better than time at the Louvre. After all, at Fauchon, the masterpieces are all there for the taking—and for the tasting.

Coffee Éclairs / Éclairs au Café

Adapted from Fauchon

In French, the word éclair means "lightning," and some people think the pastry was dubbed éclair so that its name would describe the way in which it is meant to be eaten: lightning fast. But for those of us who love an éclair's tender outside, creamy filling, and sweet glaze, lingering over it, even eating it with a knife and fork, seems the only right way. I like to think that its creator, one of the most famous chefs in French history, Antonin Carême, would agree. After all, when he invented the éclair, it was the first time that cream puff dough, pâte à choux, was given a long finger-like shape. I figure it's a sure bet that he stretched out the pastry so that we could stretch out the pleasure of eating it.

These éclairs from world-famous Fauchon (see page 128) are long, thin, and elegant, à la Carême, and filled with an espresso-flavored pastry cream that is not just traditional (coffee and chocolate have become the flavors of choice among éclair makers), but fitting to Fauchon, a company with a long history in the coffee trade. The éclairs' tops are glazed with what the pastry chef calls fondant au café, or what we Americans know as confectioners' sugar icing, a quick mix of confectioners' sugar, espresso, and a squirt of lemon juice. It's a glaze put together at éclair speed.

FAUCHON

1. **TO MAKE AND BAKE THE CREAM PUFF DOUGH**: Position the racks to divide the oven into thirds and preheat the oven to 375°F (190°C). Line two baking sheets with parchment paper and keep them close at hand. Fit a large pastry bag with a large star tip and keep this nearby as well.

2. Bring the milk, water, butter, sugar, and salt to a rapid boil in a heavy-bottomed medium saucepan over high heat. Add the flour all at once, lower the heat to medium-low, and quickly start stirring energetically with a wooden spoon. The dough will come together and a light crust will form on the bottom of the pan. Keep stirring—with vigor—for another 2 minutes to dry the dough. The dough should now be very smooth.

3. Turn the dough into the bowl of a mixer fitted with the paddle attachment or, if you're feeling strong, continue by hand. Add the eggs one by one and beat, beat, beat until the dough is thick and shiny. Don't be concerned if the dough falls apart—by the time the last egg goes in, the dough will come together again. Once the eggs have been incorporated, the still-warm dough must be used immediately.

4. Spoon half of the dough into the pastry bag and pipe out thin fingers of dough that are each about 5 inches (12 cm) long and about 1 inch (2.5 cm) wide onto the lined baking sheets, making sure to leave about 2 inches (5 cm) puff space between them. Repeat with the remaining dough.

5. Slide the baking sheets into the oven and bake for 8 minutes before slipping the handle of a wooden spoon into the oven to keep the door slightly ajar. When the éclairs have baked for 12 minutes, rotate the pans front to back and top to bottom. Continue baking until the éclairs are golden, firm, and, of course, puffed, another 8 minutes or so (the total baking time is about 20 minutes). Transfer the éclairs to a rack and cool to room temperature. *(The éclairs can be kept in a cool, dry place for several hours before filling. Alternatively, you can pipe out the éclairs and freeze them for up to 1 month before you bake them. There's no need to defrost the frozen éclairs; just bake them for a couple minutes more.)*

6. **TO FILL THE ÉCLAIRS**: Lightly whisk the espresso into the pastry cream. Carefully cut the éclairs horizontally in half (a natural cut line can be found at the puff point of each éclair); lift off the tops. Spoon the pastry cream into a pastry bag fitted with a plain tip and fill each éclair base with cream, or do this with a spoon. (You will have pastry cream left over; it can be refrigerated for up to 3 days.) Tuck the filled bases into the refrigerator, covered lightly with wax paper.

THE CREAM PUFF DOUGHTHE CREAM PUFF DOUGH

½ cup (125 grams) whole milk

½ cup (125 grams) water

1 stick (4 ounces; 115 grams) un-salted butter

Pinch of sugar

Pinch of salt

1 cup (140 grams) all-purpose flour

5 large eggs, at room temperature

THE COFFEE PASTRY CREAM

⅓ cup (80 grams) espresso, cooled

Vanilla Pastry Cream (page 179), chilled

THE COFFEE FONDANT

¼ cup (60 grams) espresso, cooled

Approximately 3 cups (600 grams) confectioners' sugar, sifted

A squirt of lemon juice

7. **TO MAKE THE FONDANT:** Pour the espresso into a small bowl. Add about 2 cups of the sifted confectioners' sugar little by little, stirring constantly with a whisk and trying not to create bubbles. Stir in the lemon juice, then continue to add as much additional confectioners' sugar as needed to produce a fondant that evenly coats the top of an éclair and stays where it is spread.

8. **TO FINISH:** One by one, hold the éclair tops over the bowl of fondant and, working with a small icing spatula, spread them with fondant. Settle each éclair top on a filled base and refrigerate the éclairs for at least 1 hour before serving.

KEEPING: The éclair shells can be frozen for up to 1 month before baking, and the pastry cream can be made up to 3 days ahead; however, the filled and glazed éclairs are best served the day they are made.

AN AMERICAN IN PARIS: Sometimes I use half the dough to make éclairs and the other half to pipe out cream puffs. The puffs are wonderful filled with pastry cream, but I often turn them into profiteroles, filling them with good store-bought ice cream and topping them with good store-bought hot fudge sauce. If I've piped the puffs ahead of time and put them in the freezer, they become a just-about-instant dessert.

Fresh Strawberry and Orange-Flower Water Marshmallows /

Guimauve Fraîche Parfumée à la Fleur d'Oranger et aux Fraises

Adapted from Ladurée

MAKES ABOUT 2¼ POUNDS
(1 KILO) MARSHMALLOWS

This recipe was given to me by Philippe Andrieu, the executive pastry chef of Paris's most romantic pâtisserie, Ladurée (see page 96). At Ladurée, the pretty pink puffs, flavored with fresh strawberry purée and a splash of orange-flower water, are used to finish the shop's delectable strawberry tart (page 98), but it almost goes without saying that the marshmallows are also delectable on their own. In fact, at some of Paris's best and most expensive restaurants, marshmallows are offered as a post-dessert nibble. In luxe restaurants (as well as in fine candy shops), marshmallows are formed not in squares, as they are in America, but in long chubby lanyards, and they are displayed in tall glass apothecary jars. When they are served to you in a great restaurant, the waiter lifts up a lanyard with a pair of silver tongs and then, always with a flourish, cuts off small cubes using large shears that resemble the ones the king's tailor uses in cartoons.

I made these strawberry marshmallows for the first time when I was in Paris and I was thoroughly surprised to find that all my French friends were as shocked that I had made marshmallows à la maison as my American friends were when I repeated this act of great fun in New York. Even for the French, marshmallows don't seem doable in a home kitchen—but they are. And, what's more, they're not just fun to make but easy as well. The only special equipment you need is a large-capacity stand mixer (the bowl should hold at least 5 quarts) and a candy thermometer. After that, what you need is a bunch of marshmallow munchers, since the recipe makes just over 2 pounds. Fortunately, if you keep the marshmallows in a cool, dry place, they'll be fine for over a week.

Approximately 1 cup (100 grams) potato starch (available in the baking or kosher foods section of most supermarkets)

8 to 10 ripe strawberries (about ¾ cup; 100 grams), hulled

1⅓ cups (300 grams) cold water

2½ cups plus 2 tablespoons (525 grams) sugar

Scant ¼ cup (75 grams) light corn syrup

4 packets (3 tablespoons; 28 grams) powdered gelatin

6 large egg whites, at room temperature

1 teaspoon orange-flower water

1. Line a 12 x 17-inch (30 x 42.5-cm) baking sheet that has a 1-inch (2.5-cm) rim with parchment paper and dust the paper heavily with potato starch; keep close at hand.

2. Purée the strawberries in a blender (traditional or hand-held) or food processor. You should have a scant ½ cup (100 grams); set this aside.

3. Put ⅔ cup (150 grams) of the water, 2½ cups (500 grams) of the sugar, and all of the corn syrup into a medium saucepan and bring to the boil over medium heat, stirring just until the sugar dissolves. Once the sugar dissolves, stop stirring and continue to cook the syrup until it reaches 265°F (130°C) on a candy thermometer, a process that could take about 10 minutes.

4. Meanwhile, sprinkle the gelatin over the remaining ⅔ cup (150 grams) cold water and let soften for 5 minutes, then heat for 35 to 45 seconds in a microwave oven to liquefy (or do this stovetop); set this aside.

5. Put the egg whites in the clean, dry bowl of a mixer fitted with the whisk attachment and beat on medium-high speed until they form soft peaks. Still beating, add the remaining 2 tablespoons (25 grams) sugar and whip until the whites form firm, glossy peaks. (Make sure not to overbeat, or the peaks will go dull.)

6. As soon as the sugar syrup has come up to temperature, reduce the mixer speed to medium and add the syrup, pouring it close to the side of the bowl to avoid the spinning whisk. Using the same technique, add the dissolved gelatin. Beat for about 3 minutes to fully incorporate the syrup and gelatin.

7. Switch to a large rubber spatula and very gently fold the strawberry purée, as well as the orange-flower water, into the hot batter. Turn the batter out onto the potato starch–dusted baking sheet and spread it into one of the ends, making

sure it reaches into the corners. Continue spreading the batter, keeping it 1 inch (2.5 cm) thick: you'll probably have enough batter to make a 12-inch (30-cm) square. Lift the excess parchment paper up to meet the edge of the marshmallow batter and put something against the paper to keep it in place (a couple of spice jars or custard cups or some dried beans will do the trick). Generously dust the top of the marshmallow square with potato starch. Allow the marshmallow to cool and set in a cool, dry place, about 3 hours (they can rest overnight, if that's more convenient for you).

8. When you are ready to serve the marshmallows (or to use them for Ladurée's Strawberry Tart, page 98), cut the square into lanyards or cubes using a thin-bladed knife or large scissors. In either case, moisten and clean the blade(s) often. Cut marshmallows should be dusted all over with potato starch and the excess shaken off.

KEEPING: Dusted with potato starch, marshmallows will hold up for a week or more if you pack them in an airtight container and keep them in a cool, dry place.

AN AMERICAN IN PARIS: Of course an American would toast these, but I wouldn't suggest it. However, I would strongly suggest that you cut some small marshmallow squares and toss them on top of an ice cream sundae. If you want to change the flavor of the marshmallows, it's easily done by changing the purée: play around with raspberry, peach, mango, or apricot. (See the Source Guide, page 185, for information on where to buy ready-to-use fruit purées.)

Hot Chocolate / Chocolat Chaud

Adapted from Ladurée

Whenever friends ask for a list of things they should do in Paris, I always tell them they must go to Ladurée (see page 96) for hot chocolate—it is one of the delights of being in the city. Chocolat chaud made in the Ladurée style is unabashedly rich, luxuriously thick, textbook smooth, and the kind of delicious that forces you to stop all reasonable conversation so you can sip and murmur, "Mmmmm." It is made with bittersweet chocolate that is more bitter than sweet, and as a result, the drink is more grown-up and sophisticated than the hot cocoa we're accustomed to feeding kids after a day of sledding. In fact, at Ladurée, the hot chocolate is made by blending two different kinds of chocolate. The formula is one part chocolate with 80 percent cacao and three parts chocolate with 67 percent cacao (see page 64). Whether you blend chocolates or use a single type, there is really only one important rule to follow: use a chocolate that you enjoy eating out of hand—there isn't much in the recipe that will change the taste of the chocolate, so you should start with what you like.

A word on preparation: After the milk and chocolate are combined, the chocolat chaud is whipped to a froth using a hand-held or traditional blender. I encourage you not to skip this step because it produces the drink's memorable smoothness. In addition, I have given you a recipe that turns out 4 servings, but it is one that can be easily multiplied or divided. It is also, as you will see, one that can be made ahead and one that can be thinned a bit and served chilled.

1. **TO MAKE HOT CHOCOLATE**: Bring the milk, water, and sugar just to the boil in a medium saucepan. Remove the pan from the heat and whisk in the chocolate. The hot chocolate needs to be blended at this point. At Ladurée, this is done with a hand-held blender (also called an immersion blender). If you have this tool, leave the hot chocolate in the saucepan and whip it with the hand-held blender for 1 minute. If you don't have a hand-held blender, transfer the chocolate to a traditional blender and whip on high speed for 1 minute. The chocolate should be served immediately, while it is still very hot and frothy. Alternatively, you can pour the chocolate into a container to cool; the cooled chocolate can be reheated or served chilled. *(The chocolate can be made up to 2 days ahead and kept tightly covered in the refrigerator.)*

2. **TO REHEAT CHILLED HOT CHOCOLATE**: Working in a medium saucepan over low heat, warm the chocolate, stirring gently, just until the first bubble pops on the surface. Pull the pan from the heat, whip the chocolate for 1 minute with a hand-held blender (or in a traditional blender), and serve immediately.

3. **TO MAKE COLD HOT CHOCOLATE**: Chill the hot chocolate until it is very cold, then stir in ¾ cup (200 grams) cold milk. Whip the cold chocolate for 1 minute with a hand-held blender (or in a traditional blender). Serve the cold hot chocolate over an ice cube or two.

3 cups (750 grams) whole milk
⅓ cup (80 grams) water
⅓ cup (65 grams) sugar
6 ounces (175 grams) bittersweet chocolate, finely chopped

KEEPING: Once blended, the hot chocolate can be cooled and refrigerated in a tightly sealed jar for 2 days; reheat gently, or serve as cold hot chocolate.

AN AMERICAN IN PARIS: Cold hot chocolate makes a fabulous ice cream float. I whip the cold chocolate to a froth, pour it into a tall glass—beer glasses are great for this—and add ice cream. While the traditional go-with-chocolate flavors, like vanilla, coffee, vanilla-fudge, and chocolate in all its renditions, are always good, my favorite floatable flavor is Ben & Jerry's Cherry Garcia.

Grand Gâteaux

for

Fêtes and Feasts

Bacchus

Adapted from La Maison du Chocolat

Chefs work hard at choosing the right name for each of their creations, and it has always been my opinion that La Maison du Chocolat's master chocolatier, Robert Linxe (see page 40), got it just right when he christened this cake Bacchus. Sure, the sweet has the same demure good looks as M. Linxe's Parisian outposts of chocolate calm, but that is just the cake's façade. It is not for nothing that it is named for the god of wine and the leader of a wild orgiastic religion. Beneath its prim exterior lies a cake so sensuous it could send a hedonist's heart racing into overdrive. The cake's most strictly Bacchusian component is a handful of golden raisins soaked in a copious amount of dark rum. It also has three moist, chewy almond and cocoa cake layers, thick cushions of a ganache that borders on being a mousse, and a polished veneer of dark chocolate glaze, the finishing touch that makes the cake look so decorous at first glance. But glance again: the cake's bumpy top terrain, the result of all those raisins nestling under their soft coat of chocolate, is telling you that something extraordinary awaits.

1. **TO MAKE THE RAISINS:** At least 3 hours and up to 1 day before you plan to make the cake, immerse the raisins in hot water for about 4 minutes, until they are puffed. Drain, drop them into a small saucepan, and, stirring constantly, warm them over low heat. When the raisins are very hot, pull the pan from the heat, pour the rum over them, and, standing back, ignite the rum with a match. Swirl the pan until the flames go out, then cover and set aside. *(The raisins and rum can be kept in a covered jar at room temperature for up to 1 day.)*

2. **TO MAKE THE CAKE:** Center a rack in the oven and preheat the oven to 350°F (180°C). Line a jellyroll pan with parchment paper and set it aside. Sift together the ground almonds, confectioners' sugar, and cocoa powder and set aside too.

3. In the clean, dry bowl of a mixer fitted with the whisk attachment, beat the egg whites with the salt until they hold medium peaks. Gradually add the sugar and continue to beat until the whites are firm but still glossy. Switch to a rubber spatula and gently fold in the sifted dry ingredients.

4. Working gingerly, spread the batter over the parchment-lined baking sheet until it forms a rectangle that is approximately 10 x 12 inches (25 x 30 cm); you will have a thin layer. Slide the baking sheet into the oven and bake for 13 to 15 minutes, or until the cake is puffed, springy, and almost dry to the touch. Transfer to a rack and allow the cake to cool to room temperature on its baking sheet.

5. When the cake is cool, cover and refrigerate it for at least 2 hours or up to 1 day.

6. **TO MAKE THE GANACHE:** Put the chocolate in a heatproof bowl and place the bowl over a saucepan of simmering water; the bowl should not touch the water. Warm the chocolate only until it begins to melt, then stir and pull the bowl from the heat. Meanwhile, put half the cream in a bowl large enough to use for whipping and put it in the refrigerator. Put the other half in a saucepan and bring it to a full boil.

7. When the cream is at the boil, pour it over the chocolate. Wait for 30 seconds, then, using a whisk, gently stir until the chocolate is completely melted and smooth. Whisk in the butter and allow the ganache to rest for 5 to 10 minutes, or until it no longer feels warm to the touch.

8. Whip the chilled cream to soft peaks. Very delicately, fold the whipped cream into the ganache. Chill the ganache, stirring every few minutes, until you can spread it and have it stay where it is spread. *(The ganache can be covered and refrigerated for up to 2 days. Warm it—see Step 10—before using.)*

THE RAISINS

½ cup (2 ounces; 60 grams) loosely packed golden raisins

¼ cup (40 grams) dark rum

THE CAKE

½ cup (50 grams) ground almonds

½ cup (60 grams) confectioners' sugar

2 tablespoons (15 grams) Dutch-processed cocoa powder

3 large egg whites, at room temperature

Pinch of salt

1½ tablespoons (15 grams) sugar

THE GANACHE

7 ounces (200 grams) bittersweet chocolate, finely chopped

¾ cup (200 grams) heavy cream

3 tablespoons (1½ ounces; 40 grams) unsalted butter, at room temperature

THE GLAZE

3½ ounces (100 grams) bittersweet chocolate, finely chopped

½ cup (125 grams) whole milk

1 teaspoon light corn syrup

1 tablespoon (½ ounce; 15 grams) unsalted butter, at room temperature

9. **TO ASSEMBLE THE CAKE:** Remove the cake from the refrigerator and cut it into three rectangles, each about 3 x 8 to 10 inches (7.5 x 20 to 25 cm). Place two of the layers on a parchment-lined baking sheet. Set one-third of the ganache aside, then spread the remaining ganache evenly over the two layers on the baking sheet. Drain the raisins, pat them dry, and stud one of the layers with half of the raisins; this is the bottom layer of the cake. Place the remaining ganache-covered layer (ganache side up) on the raisin layer and top with the remaining cake layer. Refrigerate the cake for at least 1 hour, or freeze it for about 20 minutes, to get it ready for finishing.

10. When the cake is cold, remove it from the refrigerator or freezer. If the remaining ganache has firmed and is difficult to spread, gently warm it over a pan of simmering water or give it a couple of seconds in the microwave to bring back its smooth consistency. Cover the top and sides of the cake with the ganache. Dot the top of the cake with the remaining raisins and return it to the refrigerator to set for at least 1 hour, preferably longer. (You want the ganache to be firmly set because you will be pouring hot glaze over it.) Or, again, if you are in a hurry, you can freeze the cake for 20 minutes before proceeding. *(The cake can be chilled and then, when firm, wrapped in plastic film and kept refrigerated overnight.)*

11. **TO GLAZE THE CAKE:** Before you prepare the glaze, remove the cake from the refrigerator and put it on a cooling rack placed over the paper-lined baking sheet. Put the chopped chocolate in a heatproof bowl and place it over a saucepan of simmering water; the bowl should not touch the water. Warm the chocolate only until it begins to melt, then stir and pull the bowl from the heat.

12. Bring the milk to a full boil and pour it over the chocolate. Wait for 30 seconds, then, using a whisk, gently stir until the chocolate is completely melted and smooth. Gently whisk in the corn syrup, followed by the softened butter. While the glaze is still warm, pour it evenly over the top of the cake. Tilt the cake so that the excess glaze runs off, then use a metal spatula to smooth glaze over the sides of the cake. If the sides are not evenly coated after you've poured over all of the glaze, just use the spatula to lift some of the glaze off the baking sheet and onto the cake. Return the cake to the refrigerator to set the glaze, a matter of minutes. The cake is now ready to serve, although it is best to cover it and keep it in the refrigerator for a few hours or overnight so that the different elements have a chance to mellow and blend with one another.

KEEPING: Each of the cake's elements can be made ahead. Once assembled, the cake can be refrigerated for a day or wrapped airtight and frozen for up to 1 month; defrost, still wrapped, overnight in the refrigerator.

AN AMERICAN IN PARIS: I've found that the fruit in this cake is deliciously variable. Depending on your whim, you can replace the rum-soaked raisins with tiny cubes of dried apricots (rum or an orange liqueur would be a good soaking spirit), dried cherries (soaked in kirsch or port), or even pieces of moist, winy prunes (soaked in Armagnac).

DALLOYAU If cashmere and fur were cookies and cakes, they'd feel right at home in any of the Dalloyau pastry shops, of which, thankfully for those of us who need a steady supply of their sweets, there are seven. Each shop is different, but all have the luster of *luxe*. They're the kind of place I always wanted to be taken to as a kid because they would make me feel so grown-up and so sure that being a grown-up would be delicious in every way.

Take the shop on the rue du Faubourg Saint-Honoré, for example. It is Dalloyau's flagship boutique and a veritable department store of delicacies. There are the counters with the savories, the foie gras terrines, the salads, the quiches and vegetable tarts, and the small *bouchées,* or canapés, to serve with flutes of champagne. And the counters with the chocolates, all those bonbons lined up for the picking and packing in beautifully designed boxes. And the separate counter for the *macarons* (see page 122), the sweet by which a pastry chef's reputation can be made or broken. Here, where the *macarons* are, as the French would say, "top *niveau,*" or top drawer, they come in the pastel colors of Easter eggs and the lush shades of chocolate and coffee. And there are the display counters for the tarts and cakes, the creations that have sustained Dalloyau's name since its founding in the nineteenth century.

But that's not all, for there is the tea salon/restaurant upstairs. Climb what look like chocolate steps dotted with the same gold-leaf lozenges that top Dalloyau's famous Opera Cake (page 146), and you come to the *salon de thé,* all raspberry-and-butter-colored chic, with plenty of room to stow whatever you've bought along the *rue* and plenty of restorative treats to send you back on your spree.

Several of the shops have tea salons, and all of them provide a stylish setting in which to savor the work of Dalloyau's outstanding executive pastry chef, Pascal Niau. For the past three decades, M. Niau has been the man responsible for maintaining the quality of the *maison*'s classics and for designing annual collections of new desserts. M. Niau, who has earned the right to trim his pastry chef's jacket with the blue, white, and red collar that proclaims him a *Meilleur Ouvrier de France* (Best Artisan in France), is an artist in many media. In addition to creating chocolate and sugar sculptures, he is an accomplished painter and a fine draftsman.

One afternoon, I sat with the chef and talked about his work. As he described a dessert, he would sketch it on his pad, showing it in cross section, detailing a decoration or drawing in something that hinted at its creaminess or crunch. As we finished our session, I was wildly tempted to scoop up the sketches that were scattered across the polished tabletop, feeling about them the way café keepers on the boulevard Montparnasse must have felt about the doodles the artists of the 1920s left on scrunched-up napkins. As tempting as it was, I didn't take the sketches, but I was easily consoled for the loss, since everything that had been drawn—and so much more—was available just down those bittersweet chocolate steps.

$\mathcal{O}$pera $\mathcal{C}$ake / L'Opéra

Adapted from Dalloyau

It is hard to say who invented the opera cake. Some say there was an opera cake sold in Paris as long ago as 1890, and some say it was created closer to 1950. But the point about which there is no controversy is that the greatest opera cake is made at Dalloyau (see page 144), une grande maison that cossets the classics. There, Chef Pascal Niau makes a cake as sleek and smooth as an opera stage and as gloriously delicious as La Bohème is affectingly beautiful.

The classic opéra is a work in six acts. There are three thin layers of almond cake, each soaked in a potent coffee syrup; a layer of espresso-flavored butter-cream; a layer of bittersweet chocolate ganache; and a topping of chocolate glaze. Traditionally the cake is decorated with its name written in glaze across the top and finished with a piece of shimmering gold leaf. It is obviously a rich cake, but it is surprisingly not a filling cake, and I'm convinced this is because Maestro Niau has orchestrated the cake's elements so perfectly.

A word on size: This recipe makes a square cake that is an impressive 10 inches (25 cm) on a side. Even if this is more cake than you need, it's best not to cut down the recipe. Instead, make the full cake, fill it, glaze it, cut it into smaller-sized cakes, and store them in your freezer.

THE CAKE

- 6 large egg whites, at room temperature
- 2 tablespoons (30 grams) granulated sugar
- 2 cups (225 grams) ground blanched almonds
- 2 cups (225 grams) confectioners' sugar, sifted
- 6 large eggs
- ½ cup (70 grams) all-purpose flour
- 3 tablespoons (1½ ounces; 45 grams) unsalted butter, melted and cooled

1. **TO MAKE THE CAKE:** Position the racks to divide the oven into thirds and preheat the oven to 425°F (220°C). Line two 12½ x 15½-inch (31 x 39-cm) jelly-roll pans with parchment paper and brush with melted butter (this is in addition to the quantity in the ingredient list).

2. Working in the clean, dry bowl of a mixer fitted with the whisk attachment, beat the egg whites until they form soft peaks. Add the granulated sugar and beat until the peaks are stiff and glossy. If you do not have another mixer bowl, gently scrape the meringue into another bowl.

3. In the mixer fitted with the paddle attachment, beat the almonds, confectioners' sugar, and eggs on medium speed until light and voluminous, about 3 minutes. Add the flour and beat on low speed only until it disappears. Using a rubber spatula, gently fold the meringue into the almond mixture, then fold in

the melted butter. Divide the batter between the pans and spread it evenly to cover the entire surface of each pan.

4. Bake the cake layers for 5 to 7 minutes, or until they are lightly browned and just springy to the touch. Put the pans on a heatproof counter, cover each with a sheet of parchment or wax paper, turn the pans over, and unmold. Carefully peel away the parchment, then turn the parchment over and use it to cover the cakes. Let the cakes cool to room temperature. *(The cakes can be made up to 1 day ahead, wrapped, and kept at room temperature.)*

5. **TO MAKE THE SYRUP:** Stir the water, sugar, and coffee together in a small saucepan and bring to the boil. Remove from the heat and cool. *(The syrup can be covered and refrigerated for up to 1 week.)*

6. **TO MAKE THE BUTTERCREAM:** Make a coffee extract by dissolving the instant espresso in the boiling water; set aside.

7. Bring the sugar, water, and vanilla bean pulp to a boil in a small saucepan, stirring just until the sugar dissolves. Continue to cook without stirring until the syrup reaches 255°F (124°C), as measured on a candy or instant-read thermometer; pull the pan from the heat. While the syrup is heating, put the egg and yolk in the bowl of a mixer fitted with the whisk attachment and beat until pale and foamy.

8. When the sugar syrup is at temperature, reduce the mixer speed to low and slowly pour in the syrup down the side of the bowl, doing your best to avoid the spinning whisk. Inevitably, some syrup will spin onto the sides of the bowl—don't try to stir the spatters into the eggs. Raise the speed to medium-high and continue to beat until the eggs are thick, satiny, and at room temperature, about 5 minutes.

9. Working with a rubber spatula, beat the butter until it is soft and creamy but not oily. With the mixer on medium speed, steadily add the butter in 2-tablespoon (30-gram) chunks. When all the butter has been added, raise the speed to high and beat until the buttercream is thickened and satiny. Beat in the coffee extract. Chill the buttercream, stirring frequently, until it is firm enough to be spread and stay where it is spread when topped with a layer of cake, about 20 minutes. *(The buttercream can be packed airtight and refrigerated for 4 days or frozen for 1 month; bring it to room temperature before using, then beat to smooth it.)*

10. **TO MAKE THE GANACHE:** Put the chocolate in a medium bowl and keep it close at hand. Bring the milk and cream to a full boil, pour it over the choco-

THE COFFEE SYRUP

½ cup (125 grams) water

⅓ cup (65 grams) sugar

1½ tablespoons (7 grams) instant espresso or coffee powder

THE COFFEE BUTTERCREAM

2 tablespoons (10 grams) instant espresso or coffee powder

2 tablespoons (15 grams) boiling water

1 cup (100 grams) sugar

¼ cup (60 grams) water

Pulp of ¼ vanilla bean (see page 29)

1 large egg

1 large egg yolk

1¾ sticks (7 ounces; 200 grams) unsalted butter, at room temperature

THE GANACHE

8 ounces (240 grams) bittersweet chocolate, finely chopped

½ cup (125 grams) whole milk

¼ cup (60 grams) heavy cream

4 tablespoons (2 ounces; 60 grams) unsalted butter, at room temperature

late, and wait 30 seconds, then stir gently until the ganache is smooth and glossy.

11. Beat the butter until it is smooth and creamy, then stir it into the ganache in two to three additions. Refrigerate the ganache, stirring every 5 minutes, until it thickens and is spreadable, about 20 minutes. *(The ganache can be packed airtight and refrigerated for up to 3 days or frozen for 1 month; bring to room temperature before using.)*

12. **TO ASSEMBLE THE CAKE**: Line a baking sheet with parchment or wax paper. Working with one sheet of cake at a time, cut and trim each one so that you have two pieces: one 10-inch (25-cm) square and one 10 x 5-inch (25 x 12.5-cm) rectangle. Place one square of cake on the baking sheet and moisten the layer with coffee syrup. Spread about three-quarters of the coffee buttercream evenly over the cake. (If the buttercream is soft, put the cake in the freezer for about 10 minutes before proceeding.) Top with the two rectangular pieces of cake, placing them side by side to form a square; moisten with syrup. Spread the ganache over the surface, top with the last cake layer, and moisten with syrup. Chill the cake in the freezer for about 10 minutes.

13. Cover the top of the cake with a thin layer of coffee buttercream. (This is to smooth the top and ready it for the glaze—so go easy.) Refrigerate the cake for at least 1 hour or for up to 6 hours; it should be cold when you pour over the glaze. Or if you're in a hurry, pop the cake into the freezer for about 20 minutes, then continue.

THE CHOCOLATE GLAZE
1 stick (4 ounces; 115 grams) unsalted butter
5 ounces (150 grams) bittersweet
   chocolate, finely chopped

14. **TO GLAZE THE CAKE**: Bring the butter to a boil in a small saucepan. Remove the pan from the heat and clarify the butter by spooning off the top foam and pouring the clear yellow butter into a small bowl; discard the milky residue at the bottom of the pan. Melt the chocolate in a bowl set over—not touching—simmering water, then stir in the clarified butter.

15. Lift the chilled cake off the parchment-lined pan and place it on a rack. Put the rack on the parchment-lined pan and pour the glaze over the cake, using a long offset spatula to help smooth it evenly across the top. Slide the cake into the refrigerator to set the glaze and chill the cake; it should be served slightly chilled. At serving time, using a long thin knife that you dip in hot water and wipe dry between each cut, carefully trim a thin slice from the sides of the cake so that the drips of glaze are removed and the layers revealed.

KEEPING: Each element of the cake can be made ahead, as can the assembled cake. The cake can be kept in the refrigerator, away from foods with strong odors, for 1 day, or you can freeze it, wrap it airtight once it is frozen, and then keep it frozen for 1 month; defrost, still wrapped, overnight in the refrigerator.

AN AMERICAN IN PARIS: I rarely play around with this classic, but when I do, it's to add a little crunch to the mix by pressing toasted sliced almonds into both the buttercream and the ganache.

PÂTISSERIE STOHRER

I can't remember ever being on the rue Montorgueil when it was not busy, when it was not near impossible to see the street's white, swirly, snail-like paving stones for the feet of fellow food lovers or for those of the hip and chic who work and shop along the nearby rue Étienne Marcel and come to the rue Montorgueil to lunch at its small cafés and indulge in the sweets at Pâtisserie Stohrer, Paris's oldest pastry shop.

The rue Montorgueil, just at the base of the majestic church of Saint-Eustache and only steps from what was once the most active food market in France, Les Halles, was, even in 1730, when Nicolas Stohrer set up shop, a bustling street. It was the depot for stagecoaches going to Creil and Gisors, the end of the line for oysters coming from the north, and, with the establishment of Stohrer's pâtisserie, the destination for *le Tout Paris*.

It's fun to imagine the fuss Nicolas Stohrer must have created when he established his little shop in Paris after having been the pastry chef to one of the world's great gourmands, Stanislas Leszczynski, the exiled king of Poland, and later the *chef-pâtissier* at Versailles to France's King Louis XV. Of course, Stohrer's reputation preceded him to Paris and, of course, *la crème de la crème* of Parisian society rushed to savor what he had served at court.

For me, it's a thrill to follow in the footsteps of these eighteenth-century pastry patrons. If I stand across the street from the pastry shop and squint just a little, I can see what the deep French-blue shop, with its brilliant gold lettering, mirrored panels, and sunflower-yellow awning, must have appeared like then. And how lovely the women in their full skirts and fancy bonnets must have looked as they lined up and peered into the windows, waiting their turn to buy the once-royal sweets.

It is just as thrilling to know that the shop's exterior is protected by the French historical registry, so generations to come will be able to squint and imagine the past too. As for the interior, it has been redecorated many times, but is now protected by M. Pierre Liénard, the shop's owner, who is justly proud of being in possession of such a little jewel and determined to preserve its treasures, among them the lyrical 1824 paintings by Baudry, the wonderful old turquoise-blue tile floor, and, of course, the pastries.

I am incapable of leaving Stohrer without buying the pastries of the past, the triplets of babas—*baba au rhum,* Ali-Baba (page 112), and *baba chantilly*—created for King Stanislas to commemorate his love of the *1001 Tales of the Arabian Nights;* the cream-filled puff pastries called *puits d'amour;* or the kouglofs. But I always remember M. Liénard saying to me, "We are a shop that keeps up with the times," so I also buy something new and am never disappointed: Stohrer's fruit tarts, particularly their berry tarts, are perfection; their cookies, a teatime pleasure; and their chocolate cakes, splendid. Carrying home the carefully tied blue-and-white box, I can't help thinking that I'm carrying home a time capsule, a mini lesson in the history of French gastronomy. I also can't help thinking that if all history lessons had been this delicious, school would have been so much more delightful.

Chocolate-Thyme Cake / Gâteau Chocolat-Thym

Adapted from Pâtisserie Stohrer

Stohrer (see page 150), established on the beautiful rue Montorgueil market street in 1730, is Paris's oldest pastry shop. Today, beneath Baudry's wistful paintings, classics created by Nicolas Stohrer, the shop's original pastry chef, are displayed alongside such modern-day delights as tropical fruit tarts, ganache-filled bonbons, and this unusual dessert, a downy chocolate cake filled with a layer of bittersweet chocolate mousse and a cushion of cream discreetly flavored with fresh thyme and reminiscent of the filling for a Boston cream pie. M. Liénard, Stohrer's current owner, is particularly proud of this cake because, as he said, "It shows how our very old pâtisserie keeps up with the times." Of course, he's right. But the cake also shows how simply delicious the unexpected combination of chocolate and thyme can be.

At Stohrer, the cake is finished with a thin coating of chocolate glaze. If you want a glaze, use the one on page 148; however, at home, I like to serve the cake as is, with just a dusting of cocoa on top; I love showing off the ribbons of color the cake's layers make.

THE CAKE

½ cup (70 grams) all-purpose flour

¼ cup (25 grams) Dutch-processed cocoa powder

¼ teaspoon double-acting baking powder

¼ teaspoon baking soda

3 large eggs

½ cup (100 grams) sugar

3 tablespoons (1½ ounces; 45 grams) unsalted butter, melted and cooled

1. **TO MAKE THE CAKE:** Center a rack in the oven and preheat the oven to 350°F (180°C). Butter an 8 x 2-inch (20 x 5-cm) round cake pan, line the bottom with a circle of parchment or wax paper, butter the paper, and dust the entire interior with flour, tapping out the excess.

2. Sift together the flour, cocoa, baking powder, and baking soda and set aside.

3. Whisk the eggs and sugar together in the metal bowl of a mixer (or in another heatproof bowl). Place the bowl in a large skillet filled with a few inches of hot water. Working over medium-high heat and whisking without stop, beat the eggs and sugar until they are foamy and just warm to the touch, about 4 minutes. Remove the bowl from the skillet, attach it to the mixer, fit the mixer with the whisk attachment, and beat on high speed until the mixture is cool and at least doubled in volume, about 5 minutes. When you lift the whisk, the mixture should fall back into the bowl in a slowly dissolving ribbon. Switch to a rubber spatula and gently and gradually fold in the sifted dry ingredients. When the dry ingredients are no longer visible, gently fold in the melted butter.

4. Scrape the batter into the prepared pan and bake for 20 to 22 minutes, or until the cake is springy to the touch. Transfer the cake to a rack to cool for 5 minutes, then run a blunt knife between the cake and the sides of the pan, invert the cake onto another cooling rack, remove the paper, and invert again onto the first rack. Cool to room temperature. *(The cake can be wrapped airtight and kept at room temperature for 3 days or frozen for 1 month.)*

5. **TO MAKE THE SYRUP:** Put the water, sugar, and thyme in a small saucepan and stir over high heat until the sugar dissolves. Bring to the boil, pull from the heat, and cool. Discard the thyme. *(The syrup—minus the thyme sprigs—can be covered and refrigerated for up to 1 week.)*

6. **TO MAKE THE THYME CREAM:** Bring the milk, cream, 2 tablespoons of the sugar, and the thyme to a full boil in a medium saucepan. Stir to dissolve the sugar, turn off the heat, and let infuse for at least 10 minutes or for up to 1 hour (if necessary, reheat until hot before using.) Meanwhile, sprinkle the gelatin over the cold water. When it is soft and spongy, heat it for 15 seconds in a microwave oven to liquefy (or do this stovetop); set aside.

7. Whisk together the yolks and the remaining 2 tablespoons sugar in a small bowl. Still whisking, strain the hot thyme liquid over the yolks (discard the thyme), then pour everything back into the saucepan. Stirring constantly, cook over medium heat until the cream reaches 180°F (82°C) on an instant-read thermometer, or until it coats a spoon—when you run your finger down the back of the spoon, the track you create should remain. Strain the cream into a clean bowl, stir in the dissolved gelatin, and chill, stirring frequently, just until it thickens ever so slightly. Once the cream begins to show signs of thickening, pull it out of the refrigerator and keep it at room temperature while you make the mousse. (When you are ready to use the cream, it should be part pourable, part spreadable, like the mousse.)

8. **TO MAKE THE MOUSSE:** Put the chocolate in a medium bowl. Bring ½ cup of the cream to a full boil and pour it over the chocolate. Wait a minute, then gently stir until the chocolate is smooth and glossy. Cool the ganache, stirring occasionally, 10 to 15 minutes, or until it no longer feels warm to the touch.

9. Meanwhile, whip the remaining cream until it forms soft peaks. Stir a couple of tablespoons of whipped cream into the cooled ganache, then gently fold in the rest.

THE THYME SYRUP
¾ cup (180 grams) water
½ cup (100 grams) sugar
5 sprigs fresh thyme

THE THYME CREAM
½ cup (125 grams) whole milk
½ cup (125 grams) heavy cream
¼ cup (50 grams) sugar
5 sprigs fresh thyme (or more or less according to your taste)
1¼ teaspoons powdered gelatin
2 tablespoons (30 grams) cold water
3 large egg yolks

THE CHOCOLATE MOUSSE
3½ ounces (100 grams) bittersweet chocolate, finely chopped
1 cup (250 grams) heavy cream

10. **TO ASSEMBLE THE CAKE**: Line the bottom of an 8-inch (20-cm) springform pan with parchment paper. Using a serrated knife, cut a thin slice off the top of the cake to level it; cut the cake horizontally in half. Put the bottom cake layer into the ring, cut side up (if needed, trim the layer to fit the pan), and brush with enough syrup to moisten it well. Spread the thyme cream evenly over the cake, making sure to spread it all the way to the edges, then top with the other layer of cake. Moisten the cake with syrup (you may have syrup left over) and top with the mousse, spreading it smoothly. Chill the cake for at least 2 hours.

11. If the cake is very cold, let it stand at room temperature for about 30 minutes before serving. Unmold the cake and transfer it to a serving platter. (The easiest way to unmold this cake is to warm the sides of the springform pan with a hairdryer before undoing the latch.)

KEEPING: The cake can be kept in the refrigerator, away from foods with strong odors, for 1 day or wrapped airtight and frozen for up to 1 month. Defrost overnight in the refrigerator.

AN AMERICAN IN PARIS: Instead of plain thyme in the syrup and cream, I sometimes use lemon thyme, lemon verbena, or peppermint.

Chocolate Temptation / Tentation

Adapted from Ladurée

I've come to think of this cake as "the ooh-là-là dessert" because the first time I made it—it capped a dinner for slim fashionable women in Paris—I brought it out to a chorus of ooh-là-làs. I know that "ooh-là-là" is not an extraordinary response to the arrival of dessert, especially if the dessert is homemade, as it rarely is in Paris, where great pâtisseries are plentiful. But, while I might concede an ooh-là-là or two to politesse, there is no doubt that the requests for seconds were sheer childish delight. The cake lived up to its name: it was an irresistible temptation.

This cake is also as elegant as Ladurée (see page 96), the pâtisserie in which it was created. It is a tall layer cake, almost American in its looks but completely French in its conception, composition, and refined good taste. For this cake, pastry chef Philippe Andrieu starts with a light but richly flavored cocoa cake that is cut into three layers. Each layer gets saturated with a chocolate syrup—think of it as bathing the cake in hot cocoa—spread with raspberry jam (choose one that has seeds; it will have more taste and more interest), and then topped with a bittersweet chocolate ganache that is made even more alluring by the addition of raspberry purée—bottled, frozen, or made from fresh berries with the zap of a blender. After the cake is constructed, it is chilled (overnight is best) and finished with a smooth chocolate glaze—and, if you want, a tousle of red raspberries.

THE CAKE

⅓ cup (30 grams) Dutch-processed cocoa powder

¼ cup (30 grams) all-purpose flour

2½ tablespoons (25 grams) potato starch (available in the baking or kosher foods section of most supermarkets)

5 large eggs, separated, at room temperature

¾ cup (150 grams) sugar

2 large egg yolks, at room temperature

5 tablespoons (2½ ounces; 70 grams) unsalted butter, melted and cooled

THE COCOA SYRUP

¾ cup (180 grams) water

½ cup (100 grams) sugar

¼ cup (25 grams) Dutch-processed cocoa powder

THE FILLING

9½ ounces (270 grams) bittersweet chocolate, finely chopped

1½ cups loosely packed (6¼ ounces; 180 grams) fresh red raspberries or ¾ cup (6¼ ounces; 180 grams) raspberry purée (see the Source Guide, page 185)

¾ cup (180 grams) heavy cream

7 tablespoons (3½ ounces; 100 grams) unsalted butter, at room temperature

About ⅓ cup (about 115 grams) best-quality red raspberry jam with seeds

1. **TO MAKE THE CAKE:** Center a rack in the oven and preheat the oven to 350°F (180°C). Butter a 9-inch (24-cm) springform pan, dust with flour, shake out the excess, and put the pan on a parchment-lined baking sheet. Sift together the cocoa, flour, and potato starch and set aside.

2. Working in a mixer fitted with the whisk attachment, beat the egg whites until they hold soft peaks. Still beating, add ¼ cup (50 grams) of the sugar in a steady stream, and continue to beat until the whites are firm but still glossy.

3. In a large mixing bowl, beat the egg yolks and the remaining ½ cup (100 grams) sugar together with a whisk until well blended and smooth. Switch to a rubber spatula and stir in one-third of the beaten whites to lighten the batter. Next, gently fold in the melted butter, followed by the sifted dry ingredients. Finally, working with a light touch, fold in the remaining egg whites.

4. Scrape the batter into the pan, slide the baking sheet into the oven, and bake for 35 to 40 minutes, or until the cake is puffed, springy to the touch, and just starting to come away from the sides of the pan. Transfer the cake to a cooling rack and, after 10 minutes, remove the sides of the pan. Invert the cake onto another rack, lift off the pan bottom, then turn the cake over onto the first rack. Cool the cake right side up on the rack. (*The cake can be wrapped airtight and kept at room temperature for a day or frozen for up to 1 month.*)

5. **TO MAKE THE SYRUP:** Put the water, sugar, and cocoa in a small saucepan and bring to the boil, then lower the heat and simmer for 10 minutes. Remove from the heat and cool. (*The syrup can be made up to 1 week ahead and kept tightly covered in the refrigerator.*)

6. **TO MAKE THE FILLING:** Place the chocolate in a heatproof bowl. If you have fresh raspberries, purée them in a blender (traditional or hand-held); you should have about ¾ cup (about 165 grams) purée. Put the purée in one small saucepan and put the heavy cream in another; bring both to a boil. When the cream is at the boil, pour it over the chocolate. Wait for 30 seconds, then, using a whisk, stir gently until the chocolate is melted and smooth. Gently whisk in the hot raspberry purée, followed by the butter. The ganache is now ready, and it should be used within about 15 minutes. (*Alternatively, you can press a piece of plastic film against the ganache to create an airtight seal and chill the ganache for up to 4 days. When you are ready to use the ganache, warm it gently over simmering water or in a microwave oven on low power.*)

7. **TO ASSEMBLE THE CAKE:** Wash, dry, and reassemble the springform pan. Bring the raspberry jam to a boil; remove from the heat.

8. Using a serrated knife, carefully cut the cake into 3 even layers. Place the bottom layer cut side up in the springform pan and moisten it with cocoa syrup (the cake should be very moist, but not wet). Spread a very thin coating of hot jam evenly over the cake. Finish this layer by pouring over one-third of the ganache. Continue building the cake this way—cake, syrup (don't worry if you don't use all the syrup), jam, and ganache—placing the last layer of cake cut side up and pouring the last third of the ganache over it. Chill the cake for at least 12 hours, preferably overnight, covering it with plastic wrap once the ganache is firm.

9. **TO GLAZE THE CAKE**: Put the chocolate in a heatproof bowl. Bring the cream, sugar, and water to a full boil, stirring to dissolve the sugar. Pour the hot cream over the chocolate and wait for 30 seconds, then stir very gently with a whisk to melt the chocolate and smooth the glaze.

10. Take the cake from the refrigerator and remove the sides of the springform pan. (The easiest way to unmold this cake is to warm the sides of the springform pan with a hairdryer before undoing the latch.) It's up to you whether you leave the cake on the pan's base or remove it. Place the cake on a cooling rack over a parchment-lined rimmed baking sheet and pour over the glaze. Using a metal spatula, smooth the glaze across the top of the cake and around the sides. If you are using raspberries, place them on top of the cake. Slide the cake into the refrigerator for about 15 minutes to set the glaze. If the cake is very cold (as it will be if you've chilled it overnight before glazing it or kept it in the refrigerator after glazing it), allow it to remain at room temperature for about 40 minutes before serving—the flavors are more intense when the cake is less cold.

THE GLAZE AND FINISH
4 ounces (115 grams) bittersweet chocolate, finely chopped
½ cup (125 grams) heavy cream
2 tablespoons (25 grams) sugar
2 tablespoons (25 grams) water
Fresh red raspberries for decoration (optional)

KEEPING: Once the cake is assembled, it needs an overnight chill, but it can also be frozen with its glaze, but without its fresh raspberry topping, for up to 1 month. Freeze until the glaze is set, then wrap the cake well. Defrost, still wrapped, overnight in the refrigerator.

AN AMERICAN IN PARIS: This cake is spectacular served in the French manner, that is, as its own course followed by espresso, but as sophisticated as it is, it is also wonderful eaten in the kid manner, that is, accompanied by a tall glass of cold milk. Just don't tell any of my French friends I suggested this.

PÂTISSERIE
ROLLET-PRADIER

aris is a city made up of twenty *arrondissements*—think of them as zip codes—arranged in a spiral starting at the Louvre and winding around to the edges of town. Oddly, although every *arrondissement* presses up against at least one other, each has its own personality. Sometimes it's the mix of stores that gives the neighborhood its flavor, sometimes the historic places, sometimes the cafés, the buildings, or even the famous people who live in them. In the seventh *arrondissement,* all these elements conspire to give the neighborhood an air that is rather *distingué.* The Seventh is home to the Musée d'Orsay, the Eiffel Tower, a clutch of ministries, the National Assembly and, just down the street from the Assembly, Pâtisserie Rollet-Pradier, the pastry shop and restaurant/ *salon de thé* that serves as the Assembly's unofficial daily canteen.

To look at Rollet-Pradier today, with its modern glass and stone façade, its trim glass and steel displays, and its tailored upstairs dining room, you would never suspect that this is a pâtisserie that has been tucked into this spot since 1859. In fact, I'm embarrassed to admit that I didn't know there was a pastry shop there until my friend cookbook author Nick Malgieri, who often stays in a hotel on the pâtisserie's street, brought me a lime Bavarian cream cake to taste. The following day, I walked to Rollet-Pradier, determined to make up for lost time.

As I stood in front of the shop's windows, looking at the polished pastries, I raised my eyes and saw a man on the other side of the glass looking at me looking at his wares. I smiled. He smiled. And I walked in, by this time grinning, because although I didn't yet know the shop, I already knew the man with the apple-red cheeks and the welcoming smile. He was Jean-Marie Desfontaines, last seen at Ladurée (see page 96), the renowned pâtisserie he directed until 1999.

M. Desfontaines, who spent years in the kitchens of Ladurée, may no longer be baking, but he knows fine pastry intimately and he told me that when he took the helm of Rollet-Pradier, he was determined to keep the classics, but also to add desserts that would match the time-honored sweets in quality. And he's done just that—deliciously.

Among the classics are the beloved *marquis au chocolat,* a dark chocolate ganache cake that rests on a layer of hazelnut meringue; the Mont-Blanc, a traditional chestnut dessert, here lightened with meringue and prepared in a ring whose center is filled with whipped cream; a sublime linzer tart; and the exquisite Blanc-manger (page 160), a rich but surpassingly light cream cake flavored with almonds and studded with berries. Sharing space with these classics are such newcomers as the Madagascar, a milk chocolate cake with bananas; croissants filled with hazelnuts and almonds; *bretzel sucre,* pretzel-like twists of puff pastry dredged in sugar and baked to a caramel crisp; and the incomparable Tarte au Citron (page 84), an unusual and powerfully flavorful tart that is made with whole lemons.

All of Rollet-Pradier's sweets, along with their breads and savories, are available in the dining room, where breakfast and lunch are served until the witching hour, the time in the afternoon when the room becomes a *salon de thé* and the sweet-tooth set settles in—quietly, of course. Not surprisingly, the clientele at Rollet-Pradier is as refined, restrained, and stately as the sweets. It's all in keeping with the neighborhood. As I said, the Seventh can be *très distingué.*

Blanc-manger

Adapted from Pâtisserie Rollet-Pradier

Larousse Gastronomique, *the bible of French cuisine, explains that* blanc-manger *(known as* blancmange *in America) may be one of the oldest desserts in the repertory, since it dates from the Middle Ages (when it was made either with honey and almonds or with the* gelée *that developed when cooking capon or veal). What it doesn't mention is that, at the start of this millennium, it is one of the most popular desserts—again. Part cream, part jelly (like a French version of panna cotta or, dare I say it, Jell-O?) and molded and served like a cake, the* blanc-manger *of today is a mixture of ground almonds and milk fortified with gelatin, smoothed with whipped cream, and often, as this one is, studded with morsels of fruit. It is a cake that can be varied with the seasons—it is excellent made with red berries in summer, pineapple or mango in winter, or premium-quality canned fruits when the greenmarkets' fruit stands are bare—and one that can be served after any meal, dressy or casual, hearty or light. At Rollet-Pradier (see page 158), the sleek pâtisserie just steps from the picturesque Place du Palais Bourbon, the* blanc-manger *is made in a traditional 8-inch (20-cm) cake pan, but you can make it in a springform if that suits you better, or even in a fancy gelatin mold, the kind with all the nooks and crannies. The cake is extremely easy to assemble and, since the gelatin and whipped cream need refrigerator time to set, perfect for parties— you can make it in the morning and serve it in the evening. It is not for nothing that the* blanc-manger *is the dessert of choice among chic Parisian newlyweds anxious to test their fledging culinary skills on something famous and foolproof.*

1. Have ready an 8 x 2-inch (20 x 5-cm) round cake pan or springform pan, preferably nonstick. Fill a large bowl with ice cubes and cold water and set out a smaller bowl that fits into this ice-water bath.

2. Sprinkle the gelatin over the cold water. When it is soft and spongy, heat it for 15 seconds in a microwave oven to liquefy it (or do this stovetop); set aside. Whip the chilled heavy cream until it holds medium-firm peaks; refrigerate.

3. Bring the milk, almonds, and sugar to a boil in a medium saucepan over medium heat, stirring occasionally to make certain the sugar dissolves. At the boil, pull the pan from the heat and stir in the dissolved gelatin, as well as the kirsch. Pour this into the set-aside small bowl and set the bowl into the ice-water bath. Stir regularly, and lift the bowl out of the ice bath as soon as the mixture cools and starts to thicken.

4. Working with a flexible rubber spatula, fold in the whipped cream. Still working with the spatula and a light touch, fold in the fruit. Scrape the *blanc-manger* into the pan and refrigerate for at least 2 hours or for up to 24 hours.

5. To serve, unmold the cake onto a cake plate. (If you've used a cake pan, the easiest way to unmold the *blanc-manger* is to dunk the pan into a sink full of hot water. If you've used a springform, warm the sides of the pan with a hairdryer before opening the latch.)

KEEPING: Once assembled, the *blanc-manger* can be stored in the refrigerator, away from foods with strong odors, for 1 day, although it is preferable to serve it the day it is made.

AN AMERICAN IN PARIS: During the summer, I like to make this with blueberries—wild blueberries, when I can get them. I ditch the kirsch and just flavor the mixture with a couple teaspoons of pure vanilla extract.

1 packet (2½ teaspoons; 7 grams) powdered gelatin

3 tablespoons cold water

1½ cups (375 grams) chilled heavy cream

¾ cup (200 grams) whole milk

¾ cup (100 grams) ground blanched almonds

½ cup (100 grams) sugar

2 to 3 tablespoons kirsch, or to taste

1 peach, peeled, pitted, and cut into small dice

2 slices canned or fresh pineapple, cut into small dice

½ cup (100 grams) strawberries, preferably *fraises des bois*, hulled and halved (if using larger berries, cut them into small dice)

PÂTISSERIE VANDERMEERSCH

$\mathcal{D}$epending on my métro connections, it takes about thirty minutes for me to get from my apartment in Saint-Germain-des-Prés to Pâtisserie Vandermeersch in the twelfth *arrondissement*. Even when I make better time, it isn't a cinch to reach this easternmost edge of Paris, and on my first trip, when I emerged from the station, I felt the way Alice must have felt when she finished tumbling down the rabbit hole: I didn't know where I was.

I stepped out onto a wide, airy avenue lined with trees and cafés, newsstands, and very simple restaurants. Catching a glimpse of the Bois de Vincennes just beyond a heroic gilt statue at the end of the broad street only strengthened my sense that I was a step away from crossing over the Paris border.

This part of the twelfth *arrondissement* is one you'd work in and live in, but probably not one you'd visit much either as a tourist or even as a more centrally located Parisian. At least that was true until Stéphane Vandermeersch opened his cookie-tin-sized pastry shop.

Vandermeersch is a young, serious, somewhat shy, and very talented pastry chef who says he was born with a sweet tooth and the desire to become a *pâtissier*. "After all," he told me, "when my mother was pregnant with me, she went to Lenôtre's pastry shop every day, bought a box full of *macarons* [see page 123], and ate them all herself. Those cookies must have sealed my destiny."

What sealed the little shop's destiny shortly after it opened was an article in *Le Monde* extolling the chef's mille-feuille (page 168). After the reviewer finished describing the glorious flakiness of the mille-feuille's puff pastry layers, the smoothness of the cream filling, and the perfection of the construction, connoisseurs from all over the capital made the pilgrimage to Vandermeersch's doorstep. Then, one year later, *Le Figaro* crowned Vandermeersch's *galette des rois* (page 164) the best in Paris, and the following day the line outside the shop was three hundred meters long, the length of three football fields. Vandermeersch knows the length because it was measured by the hotel owner across the street, who had never seen so many people in the neighborhood and photographed the phenomenon for posterity. That weekend, Vandermeersch sold 1,600 *galettes des rois,* as many as he expected to sell during the entire month of January, the official time for the cake, which is the most delicious part of any celebration of Epiphany.

Of course, success can be as fickle in France as it can be anywhere else, but as is always true, quality endures. Once the *galette* rush subsided, the same people who had traveled to the Twelfth to get the new best thing returned, this time to sample the fruit tarts, among them the terrific citrus tart with pistachio cream filling, the bready kouglof (page 44) soaked in orange-flower water syrup, and the filled and frosted cakes that show the pastry chef's whimsy, as well as his training in kitchens as famed as those of Fauchon (see page 128) and Ladurée (see page 96). In fact, it was at Ladurée that Stéphane Vandermeersch met his wife, who now works with him in the shop and who, when there aren't eight hundred people waiting outside the door, greets every visitor with a warmth that makes the journey worth it even before you've had your first cookie.

Kings' Cake / Galette des Rois

Adapted from Pâtisserie Stéphane Vandermeersch

It seems that no sooner do Christmas logs (bûches) disappear from pastry-shop shelves in Paris than galettes des rois, or kings' cakes, show up. Created to celebrate Epiphany, or Twelfth Night, the day the Three Kings visited the infant Jesus, the galette should probably appear only on Epiphany, January 6, but knowing something wonderful when they see (and taste) it, Parisians have made the galette des rois a *month-long indulgence.*

The word galette *can mean many things (see page 30 for a fuller explanation), among them a crêpe; a small savory pancake (think potato pancake); a cookie, usually a butter cookie from Brittany; or a round thick but not particularly high cake, like the kings' cake. The* galette des rois *is two rounds of puff pastry filled with a mixture of almond cream and pastry cream. It is as simple as it sounds. It is also preternaturally good and as much fun as a game of chance.*

In fact, the galette des rois *is as much game as it is* gourmandise, *since each galette is sold with a gold paper crown. Usually the cake is presented adorned with its crown. The crown is set aside when the cake is cut and then it makes a triumphant reappearance at the coronation of the lucky person whose slice of galette contains the hidden* fève, *or trinket. Fève means "bean," and perhaps it was a bean that was originally tucked into the cake, but today the trinket is more likely to be made of ceramic or porcelain. Similarly, while the early* fèves *were figures representing the Three Magi, Jesus, or the Virgin Mary, today's may be good luck charms, such as horseshoes or four-leaf clovers; pop icons (there are Concorde* fèves*); or something designed specifically by or for a pastry chef and changed each year, so that the* fève *becomes a collector's item.*

This galette des rois *comes from Stéphane Vandermeersch (see page 162), the pastry chef whom many consider the* roi of galette des rois. *One year after Vandermeersch's mille-feuille was named the best in Paris (see page 168), his* galette des rois *received the same honor from* Le Figaro. *To meet the ensuing demand, all hands were put to work on galettes (most of his non-galette sweets weren't even made for a few weeks), and extra orders for crowns and* fèves *were placed (and still the chef ended up having to borrow* fèves *from a fellow pastry chef who'd already stopped making galettes). Then, just when it looked as though life would settle into its pre-galette routine, the paper came out with another article about Vandermeersch's exceptional kings' cake, and the snaky wrap-around lines formed at the pâtisserie again.*

To get the full Vandermeersch effect, you should make the galette with Inside-Out Puff Pastry (page 182). But if making puff pastry is not on your holiday to-do list, don't give up on this—you'll produce a great galette if you use store-bought all-butter puff pastry.

14 ounces (400 grams) puff pastry, homemade (page 182) or store-bought (see the Source Guide, page 185)

¾ cup (185 grams) Almond Cream (page 178)

¼ cup (70 grams) Vanilla Pastry Cream (page 179)

1 tablespoon (15 grams) dark rum

1 large egg

1 trinket (see headnote above)

1. Line two baking sheets with parchment paper and keep them close at hand.

2. Divide the pastry in half and work with one half at a time; keep the other half in the refrigerator. Working on a floured surface, roll one piece of the puff pastry into a circle about ⅛ inch (4 mm) thick. Using a pan lid or the bottom of a tart pan, cut out a circle that is about 9 inches (24 cm) in diameter. Transfer the circle to a lined baking sheet, cover with plastic wrap, and refrigerate. Roll the second piece of pastry out in the same manner, but this time cut out a circle that is about 9½ inches (26 cm) in diameter. Place this circle on the other baking sheet, cover, and refrigerate as well.

3. Whisk the almond cream, pastry cream, and rum together in a bowl, stirring just to blend the two creams, not to whip air into them. In a small bowl, beat the egg just to break it up.

4. Remove the smaller circle of pastry from the refrigerator and paint the outer 1-inch (2.5-cm) border with a light coating of beaten egg. Spoon the almond-pastry cream mixture onto the pastry and spread it smoothly across the circle, stopping when you reach the egg-painted border. Put the trinket anywhere on top of the cream and press it in gently. Cover the cream-coated circle with the top round of puff pastry, pressing it firmly around the border to glue the two pieces together. You have a choice here: You can press the edges together with the tines of a fork to both decorate and seal them, or you can use a small sharp paring knife to create a scallop pattern all around the border. Whatever you do, the important thing is to make certain that the edges are sealed.

5. Brush the entire top of the galette with the beaten egg, then, using the tip of a paring knife, decorate the top by drawing curved lines from the center of the galette to the edges. The lines should resemble backward C's or quotation marks. Don't worry about the design—even if you make straight lines radiating from the center out, your galette will be attractive. The only important thing here is not to pierce the dough. Cut a small circle of dough, a steam vent, out of the center of the galette, slide the galette into the refrigerator, and chill it for at least 30 minutes. (*The galette can be covered and kept in the refrigerator for a day or wrapped airtight and frozen for up to 1 month.*)

6. Center a rack in the oven and preheat the oven to 475°F (250°C). (Or, if you are using store-bought puff pastry, follow the temperature instructions on the package.)

7. Slip the galette into the oven and immediately lower the temperature to 400°F (200°C). Bake the galette for 40 minutes, or until it is beautifully puffed and deeply golden brown. (If, after 20 minutes, the galette is browning too quickly,

cover it loosely with a foil tent.) Remove the galette from the oven, place the baking sheet on a cooling rack, and allow the galette to cool for 10 minutes before serving. Many consider the galette at its best when it is served hot or warm, but it is still delicious at room temperature.

KEEPING: Although the constructed galette can be chilled for a day or frozen for up to a month, once it is baked, it should be served that day.

AN AMERICAN IN PARIS: Without the trinket, the *galette des rois* becomes a version of a *Pithiviers*, another classic French dessert. For something just a little more American, instead of using the trinket, top the cream with some sautéed apples. (The apples from the Toast-Point Apple Tart, page 74, are perfect for this.)

Mille-feuille

Adapted from Pâtisserie Stéphane Vandermeersch

Mille-feuille *means "a thousand layers," a reference to the number of layers of butter and dough you end up with when you make puff pastry, and it is the name of a dessert that is better known in the United States as a napoleon. In France, the mille-feuille is a dessert that separates the good pastry chefs from the great. It is, as pastries go, relatively simple: three layers of puff pastry sandwiching two layers of pastry cream. But it is this simplicity, the fact that there's nothing to cover up the quality of the pastry or the cream, that makes the mille-feuille such a challenge to perfect. Not only has Stéphane Vandermeersch (see page 162) met that challenge, but he's got newspaper clippings to prove it:* Le Monde, *the New York Times of France, cited Vandermeersch's mille-feuille as the one to seek out in the City of Light.*

At his pâtisserie, Vandermeersch makes Inside-Out Puff Pastry (page 182), and I urge you to do the same for two reasons: one, it will be fabulous; and two, no matter how many times you make puff pastry, you will always feel tremendously self-satisfied at the finish. However, you don't have to miss the joys of this dessert because you don't have the time to make puff pastry from scratch; you can make an impeccable mille-feuille with store-bought all-butter puff pastry.

1. **TO MAKE THE CREAM:** Bring the milk and vanilla beans (pod and pulp) to a boil in a saucepan over medium heat. Cover the pan, turn off the heat, and infuse for at least 10 minutes or for up to 1 hour. (If necessary, reheat the milk until hot before continuing.)

2. Fill a large bowl with ice cubes and set aside a small bowl that can hold the finished cream and be placed in this ice bath. Set aside a fine-mesh strainer too.

3. Whisk the yolks, sugar, and cornstarch together in a heavy-bottomed medium saucepan. Whisking all the while, drizzle a quarter of the hot milk into the yolks. Still whisking, pour the rest of the liquid over the tempered yolks in a steady stream; remove and discard the pods (or save them for another use; see page 29).

4. Place the saucepan over high heat and, whisking vigorously and without stop, bring the mixture to the boil. Keep the mixture at the boil—whisking energetically—for 1 to 2 minutes, then remove the pan from the heat and press the cream through the sieve into the reserved small bowl. Set the bowl in the ice bath (you can add some cold water to the cubes now) and, stirring frequently so that the mixture remains smooth, cool the cream for about 3 minutes. (It should be 140°F [60°C], as measured on an instant-read thermometer.) Remove the bowl from the ice-water bath and stir in the butter a tablespoon at a time. Return the bowl to the ice bath and, stirring occasionally, cool completely. *(The cream can be wrapped airtight and refrigerated for 2 days.)*

5. **TO MAKE THE PASTRY:** Cut a piece of parchment paper to line a rimmed baking sheet that is about 18 x 12 inches (45 x 30 cm). Lightly moisten the parchment with a wet pastry brush.

6. Working on a floured surface, roll the puff pastry into a rectangle about 10 inches (25 cm) wide by 14 inches (35 cm) long and about ⅛ inch (4 mm) thick. Roll the dough up around your rolling pin, then unroll it onto the parchment-covered baking sheet. Cover the dough with a piece of plastic wrap and chill it for 1 to 2 hours, the time needed to allow the gluten to relax so the pastry will rise evenly and maintain its size and shape under heat.

7. Center a rack in the oven and preheat the oven to 450°F (230°C). (Or, if you are using store-bought puff pastry, follow the temperature instructions on the package.)

8. Remove the baking sheet from the refrigerator, lift off and discard the plastic wrap, and slide the baking sheet into the oven. Close the oven door, then immediately lower the oven temperature to 375°F (190°C). Bake the pastry for 8 to 10 minutes, at which point it will have risen and begun to brown. Gently

THE PASTRY CREAM

2½ cups (625 grams) whole milk

2 moist, plump vanilla beans, split and scraped (see page 29)

8 large egg yolks

¾ cup (150 grams) sugar

6½ tablespoons (55 grams) cornstarch, sifted

5 tablespoons (2½ ounces; 70 grams) unsalted butter, at room temperature

THE PASTRY

14 ounces (400 grams) puff pastry, homemade (page 182) or store-bought (see The Source Guide, page 185)

Confectioners' sugar for dusting

place a large cooling rack over the pastry—this will keep it from rising too exuberantly—and bake for another 10 to 15 minutes, or until the pastry is puffed and deeply golden. Pull the pan from the oven, lift off the cooling rack, and place the pan on a cool cooling rack. Cool for at least 1 hour.

9. **TO ASSEMBLE THE MILLE-FEUILLE:** Put the puff pastry on a large cutting board covered with a cloth towel or wax or parchment paper (to catch the many crumbs) and, using a serrated knife—or, better yet, an electric knife—and a sawing motion, cut it crosswise into 3 pieces. Spread half of the filling smoothly over one of the pieces, then top with a second piece of pastry, gently settling the pastry against the filling. Spread the remainder of the filling smoothly over this second piece of pastry and top with the third strip of pastry, again settling it into place.

10. You can present the mille-feuille as a large cake or cut the strip into 6 portions. If you decide to present the mille-feuille intact, dust it with confectioners' sugar and show it off, then take it into the kitchen to cut (since the thousand layers shatter into a million crumbs). Use an electric knife or serrated knife and a sawing motion to get the cleanest cuts.

KEEPING: Covered tightly, the pastry cream can be refrigerated for 2 days. Once the puff pastry is baked, it should be used as soon after it cools as possible, certainly the same day. Finally, it is best to assemble the mille-feuille shortly before serving time. If you can't, try to make it no more than 4 hours ahead—the puff pastry will lose some of its crispiness if it is in prolonged contact with the cream.

AN AMERICAN IN PARIS: The mille-feuille is both beautiful and delicious made in a black-and-white version, in which one layer is filled with chocolate pastry cream, the other with vanilla. The easiest way to make a chocolate pastry cream is to make the vanilla cream and divide it in half before you add the butter. Return one-half to the saucepan and stir in 3 ounces (100 grams) bittersweet chocolate, finely chopped, and 3 tablespoons (65 grams) whole milk. Bring the pastry cream back to the boil, then scrape it into a clean bowl. Divide the butter in half and stir one-half into each bowl of pastry cream. Cool and carry on.

Gâteau Saint-Honoré

Adapted from Dalloyau

This seems the perfect cake to come from Pâtisserie Dalloyau (see page 144) and Pascal Niau, its highly regarded pastry chef, since Saint-Honoré is the patron saint of pastry chefs and Dalloyau was founded—and can still be found—on the rue du Faubourg Saint-Honoré. The gâteau Saint-Honoré (funny, it is never referred to as a Saint-Honoré cake) is a grand cake in every sense of the term: It is a spectacularly beautiful, fabulously good tasting, texturally varied cake that has been a Paris sweet for more than one hundred years. It is a cake built on a round of pastry circled by cream puffs, which are filled with vanilla pastry cream and topped with a mirror-shiny caramel. The center of the cake is filled with a vanilla crème Chiboust, a mix of pastry cream and meringue that is named for the Parisian pastry chef who created it and made the gâteau Saint-Honoré famous in the late

nineteenth century. Finally, because too much of a good thing is often just the right amount, the cake is domed with whipped cream. I never make this cake without imagining that I am constructing a fairy-tale château.

Clearly, the gâteau Saint-Honoré is a cake of many parts. Fortunately, it is also a cake of many do-aheadables. You can make all the elements in advance and build the cake on the day it is to be served.

A word on decoration: The whipped cream, or chantilly, on a strictly traditional gâteau Saint-Honoré is piped using a pastry bag fitted with an eponymous Saint-Honoré tip, a tip that produces a graceful wedge shape. If you have such a tip, now is the time to bring it out; if you don't, just do what many pastry shops do, top the cake with rosettes piped through an open star tip, or make swirls of cream with the flat side of a rubber spatula. This cake is intrinsically beautiful; none of its enormous appeal depends on special decorating skill or gear.

THE CRUST

1 stick plus 5 tablespoons (7½ ounces; 180 grams) unsalted butter, at room temperature

½ teaspoon salt

½ teaspoon sugar

1 large egg

3½ tablespoons (50 grams) whole milk

1¾ cups (245 grams) all-purpose flour

THE CREAM PUFF DOUGH

½ cup (125 grams) whole milk

½ cup (125 grams) water

1 stick (4 ounces; 115 grams) unsalted butter, cut into 8 pieces

Pinch of sugar

Pinch of salt

1 cup (140 grams) all-purpose flour

5 large eggs, at room temperature

1. **TO MAKE THE CRUST:** Put the butter, salt, and sugar in the bowl of a food processor and process until the butter is soft and creamy. Add the egg and milk and pulse to blend. Add the flour and pulse in quick spurts until the dough almost forms a ball—then stop. Turn the dough out onto a smooth work surface and gather it into a ball. Cut the ball in half, flatten each half into a disk, and wrap the disks in plastic wrap. Chill the dough for at least 4 hours. *(You will need only 1 disk of dough but it is difficult to make a smaller quantity. The extra dough can be kept in the refrigerator for up to 3 days or frozen for up to 1 month.)*

2. Line a baking sheet with parchment paper and keep it close at hand. Working on a generously floured work surface, roll the dough out to a thickness of ⅛ inch (4 mm). Cut out a 10¼-inch (26-cm) circle and transfer the circle to the lined baking sheet. Cover and chill the dough while you work on the cream puffs.

3. **TO MAKE AND BAKE THE CREAM PUFF DOUGH:** Position the racks to divide the oven into thirds and preheat the oven to 375°F (190°C). Line two baking sheets with parchment paper and keep them close at hand. Fit a pastry bag with a ½-inch (1.5-cm) plain tip and keep it nearby as well.

4. Bring the milk, water, butter, sugar, and salt to a rapid boil in a heavy-bottomed medium saucepan over high heat. Add the flour all at once, lower the heat to medium-low, and quickly start stirring energetically with a wooden spoon. The dough will come together and a light crust will form on the bottom of the pan.

Keep stirring—with vigor—for another 2 minutes to dry the dough. The dough should be very smooth.

5. Scrape the dough into the bowl of a mixer fitted with the paddle attachment, or if you're feeling strong, continue by hand. Add the eggs one by one and beat, beat, beat on medium speed until the dough is thick and shiny. Don't be concerned if the dough falls apart—by the time the last egg goes in, the dough will come together again. Once the eggs are incorporated, the still-warm dough must be used immediately.

6. Spoon the dough into the pastry bag. Remove the rolled-out crust from the refrigerator, uncover it, and pipe a circle of cream puff dough around the circumference of the disk, leaving a ¼-inch (7-mm) border bare. Move the bag to the center of the disk and, working from the center out, pipe a spiral, somewhat like a snail shell. The spiral should not be very tight; its purpose is just to weight the disk down during baking. Set the disk aside for the moment.

7. Working on the second baking sheet (and using whatever space remains on the first sheet, if needed), pipe out as many small puffs as you can, making each puff only a little more than 1 inch (2.5 cm) in diameter and leaving at least 2 inches (5 cm) of space between them. (If your puffs have pointy tops, press the points down with a damp finger.) You'll need 16 to 20 puffs for the gâteau, but you'll have enough dough to make more—you can either bake the extras now or freeze them unbaked until needed. (*The puffs and the disk with puff dough can be frozen unbaked. Wrap the pastries airtight once they are frozen and freeze for up to 1 month. There's no need to defrost them—just add a couple of minutes to the baking time.*)

8. Slide the baking sheets into the oven and bake for 7 minutes, then slip the handle of a wooden spoon into the oven to keep the door slightly ajar. After 12 minutes in the oven, rotate the sheets top to bottom and front to back, then continue baking until the base and the puffs are golden brown. The puffs will need a total of 15 to 20 minutes in the oven, while the base will need about 25 minutes; remove any puffs on the sheet with the base as they are done. When baked, transfer the baking sheets to cooling racks and cool to room temperature.

9. **TO MAKE THE KIRSCH CREAM:** Whisk the pastry cream to soften and smooth it, then beat in the kirsch. Spoon the cream into a pastry bag fitted with a ¼-inch (7-mm) plain tip. Using the tip, poke a hole in the bottom of 16 to 20 cream puffs and then fill the puffs with pastry cream. Keep the puffs on the counter while you make the caramel.

THE KIRSCH PASTRY CREAM
2 cups (800 grams) Vanilla Pastry Cream (page 179), cooled
3 tablespoons kirsch, or to taste

THE CARAMEL

1¼ cups (250 grams) sugar

½ cup (125 grams) water

2½ teaspoons corn syrup

1½ teaspoons fresh lemon juice

THE CHIBOUST

½ cup (125 grams) heavy cream

¼ cup (60 grams) whole milk

½ moist, plump vanilla bean, split
and scraped (see page 29)

5 large eggs, separated

½ cup (100 grams) sugar

1½ tablespoons (12 grams) cornstarch, sifted

10. **TO MAKE THE CARAMEL AND DIP THE PUFFS:** Put the sugar, water, corn syrup, and lemon juice in a heavy-bottomed medium saucepan over medium heat. Stir to moisten the sugar, then bring to the boil, swirling the pan occasionally until the sugar dissolves. If sugar crystals form on the sides of the pan, wash them away with a pastry brush dipped in cold water. Cook until the mixture is a light caramel color, then pull the pan from the heat and stop the cooking by running the bottom of the pan under cold water for 10 seconds or by dipping it into an ice-water bath for 10 seconds. The caramel is ready to use. If you have to wait, or if while you're working the caramel cools and thickens, you can reheat it over gentle heat, swirling the pan so the caramel warms evenly.

11. Set out a nonstick baking sheet, a baking sheet lined with a Silpat or other silicone baking mat, or a well-buttered regular baking sheet. Working with one puff at a time, holding the puff gently between your fingers, dip the top of each puff into the caramel, then place, caramel side down on the baking sheet. Watch your fingers—the caramel is very hot.

12. When the caramel has hardened (a matter of seconds), bring the baked disk to the counter. Check that the caramel in the pan is still smooth-flowing (if it's not, just heat it briefly), and, one by one, dip the bottom of each puff into the caramel, then put the puffs, hot caramel side down, on the base's cream puff border. Keep dipping and "gluing" the puffs until the base is completely encircled. (If you have puffs left over, make some coffee and consider them your treat.) Put the base in the refrigerator.

13. **TO MAKE THE CHIBOUST CREAM:** Bring the cream, milk, and vanilla bean (pulp and pod) to a boil in a small saucepan over medium heat. Cover the pan, turn off the heat, and allow the milk to infuse for at least 10 minutes, or for up to 1 hour. (If necessary, reheat until hot before continuing.) Set out a fine-mesh strainer.

14. Whisk the yolks, 2 tablespoons (25 grams) of the sugar, and the cornstarch together in a heavy-bottomed medium saucepan. Whisking constantly, drizzle one-quarter of the hot milk over the yolks. When the yolks are warm, whisk the remainder of the milk into the yolks in a steadier stream; remove and discard the pod (or save it for another use; see page 29). Put the pan over medium heat and, whisking vigorously, bring the mixture to the boil. Keep at the boil—still whisking energetically—for 1 to 2 minutes. Then pull the pan from the heat and press the cream through the strainer into the small bowl.

15. In the clean, dry bowl of a mixer fitted with the whisk attachment, whip the egg whites until they hold very soft peaks. Add the remaining 6 tablespoons (75 grams) sugar in a steady stream and continue to whip until the whites hold firm, glossy peaks. Gently fold the meringue into the still-warm Chiboust cream.

16. Fill a pastry bag fitted with a ¾-inch (2-cm) plain tip (or use a spoon or a rubber spatula). Remove the base of the gâteau from the refrigerator and fill the center with the Chiboust, mounding it in the center so that it forms a dome. Return the cake to the refrigerator while you make the chantilly.

17. **TO MAKE THE CHANTILLY:** Working in a mixer fitted with the whisk attachment, beat the cream and vanilla extract until the cream holds soft peaks. Still beating, add the sugar, and continue to beat until the peaks are firm. Spoon the cream into a pastry bag fitted with a ¾-inch (2-cm) Saint-Honoré tip or an open star tip. If you have a Saint-Honoré tip, use it to pipe a chevron pattern over the dome of Chiboust cream. If you are using a star tip, cover the Chiboust with rosettes. Alternatively, you can just spread the whipped cream over the cake with a spatula. Chill the finished cake, away from foods with strong odors, for at least 1 hour before serving.

THE *CHANTILLY*

¾ cup (190 grams) chilled heavy cream

¼ teaspoon pure vanilla extract

1½ tablespoons (25 grams) sugar

KEEPING: The base, the puffs, and the creams can be made ahead, but once the gâteau is finished, it should be served within 12 hours—this is not a cake to hold.

AN AMERICAN IN PARIS: When I have wanted this cake but have not had the time to make everything as it should be made, I've taken two shortcuts. First, I've used store-bought puff pastry (see the Source Guide, page 185) instead of making a crust from scratch. Second, I've skipped the Chiboust cream and filled the center of the gâteau with the same vanilla pastry cream used to fill the puffs. To make this cream as close as possible to the Chiboust, I lighten it with a meringue (2 large egg whites whipped with 3 tablespoons sugar). If you don't tell anyone you cheated, I promise no one will know—unless you've invited Dalloyau's pastry chef, Pascal Niau, to dinner.

Base Recipes

Almond Cream / Crème d'Amande

Almond cream is a French pastry kitchen indispensable. It is often used on its own as the sole and luscious base of a fruit tart (the first really French tart I ever made had an almond-cream base, was topped with canned pear halves, and was spectacularly wonderful); it can be spread thinly across the bottom of a tart crust to add a flavorful cushion, waterproof shield, and extra layer of texture and taste; or it can be mixed with pastry cream to become a filling for a tart, cake, or galette, as it does in the Galette des Rois (page 164). Luckily for both French pastry chefs and us home bakers, almond cream is very quick and easy to make, especially if you use a food processor. In addition, the recipe can be multiplied (just about ad infinitum), and leftover cream can be refrigerated or frozen.

6 tablespoons (3 ounces; 85 grams) unsalted butter, at room temperature

¾ cup (85 grams) confectioners' sugar

¾ cup (85 grams) ground blanched almonds

2 teaspoons all-purpose flour

1 teaspoon cornstarch

1 large egg, at room temperature

To make the almond cream in a food processor, fit the processor with the metal blade, add the butter and confectioners' sugar, and process until the mixture is smooth and satiny. Add the ground almonds and continue to process until well blended. Add the flour and cornstarch and process, then add the egg. Process for about 15 seconds more, or until the almond cream is homogeneous. If you prefer, you can make the cream in a mixer fitted with the whisk attachment or in a bowl with a rubber spatula. In either case, the ingredients are added in the same order. Scrape the almond cream into a container and use immediately or refrigerate until firm.

KEEPING: The almond cream can be packed airtight and kept in the refrigerator for up to 4 days or frozen for up to 1 month. Defrost, still wrapped, overnight in the refrigerator, then beat it with a spatula or spoon to bring it back to its original consistency.

AN AMERICAN IN PARIS: I know that almond cream is supposed to be made with blanched almonds, but so often my pantry has nothing but almonds with their skins on. I could boil the almonds, skin, toast, then cool and grind them—but I don't. I just go ahead and grind the almonds skin and all. No one has ever complained.

Vanilla Pastry Cream I

Crème Pâtissière à la Vanille

MAKES ABOUT 2 CUPS
(800 GRAMS)

Perfect pastry cream (and this cream is perfect) is smooth and satiny, firm enough to stand up as a layer in a tart or cake, and luxurious enough to tempt you to eat it by the spoonful. No matter what flavor pastry cream you want, it is always good to start with this vanilla cream. Vanilla rounds out the flavor of the cream and gets it ready for anything else you might do with it. Although vanilla beans give the best flavor, you'll still get a great cream if you use 1 tablespoon pure vanilla extract instead of the bean. If you use extract, add it after you've stirred in the butter.

2 cups (500 grams) whole milk

1 moist, plump vanilla bean, split and scraped (see page 29)

6 large egg yolks

½ cup (100 grams) sugar

⅓ cup (45 grams) cornstarch, sifted

3½ tablespoons (1¾ ounces; 50 grams) unsalted butter, cut into 3 pats, at room temperature

1. Bring the milk and vanilla bean (pulp and pod) to a boil in a small saucepan over medium heat. Cover the pan, turn off the heat, and allow the milk to infuse for at least 10 minutes, or for up to 1 hour. (If necessary, reheat the milk until hot before proceeding.)

2. Fill a large bowl with ice cubes and set aside a smaller bowl that can hold the finished cream and be placed in this ice bath. Set aside a fine-mesh strainer too.

3. Whisk the yolks, sugar, and cornstarch together in a heavy-bottomed medium saucepan. Whisking constantly, drizzle one-quarter of the hot milk over the yolks. When the yolks are warm, whisk the remainder of the milk into the yolks in a steadier stream; remove and discard the pod (or save it for another use; see page 29).

4. Put the pan over medium heat and, whisking vigorously, bring the mixture to the boil. Keep at the boil—still whisking energetically—for 1 to 2 minutes, then pull the pan from the heat and press the cream through the strainer into the small bowl. Set the bowl into the ice bath (you can add some cold water now) and, stirring frequently, cool the cream to 140°F (60°C).

5. Remove the cream from the ice-water bath and whisk in the butter. Return the cream to the ice-water bath and keep it there until it is thoroughly chilled.

KEEPING: Covered tightly with plastic wrap (press the plastic against the cream's surface to create an airtight seal), pastry cream can be refrigerated for 2 days. To smooth the chilled cream, whisk it for a few seconds.

Sweet Tart Dough / Pâte Sucrée

This is a classic sweet tart dough, the one pastry chefs learn as apprentices. It is really a cookie dough—in fact, it is used as the base of the Orange Galettes (page 30)—and it is perfect with any sweet tart, whether the filling is fruit, ganache, or custard.

The easiest way to make this dough is in a large-capacity food processor, although it can be made quickly in a mixer fitted with the paddle attachment. Whichever method you choose, just make certain to go easy on the dough—its lovely texture depends on your not overworking the flour. Finally, as you'll see, this is a large recipe—enough for three crusts. With a dough like this, the texture is always better if you make a large batch, so it's best not to cut the proportions; rather, make the full recipe and freeze the dough you don't need at the moment: Frozen tart dough is always a good thing to have on hand.

2½ sticks (10 ounces; 290 grams) unsalted butter, at room temperature

1½ cups (150 grams) confectioners' sugar, sifted

Lightly packed ½ cup (2¼ ounces; 70 grams) ground blanched almonds

½ teaspoon salt

½ teaspoon pure vanilla extract

2 large eggs, at room temperature

3½ cups (490 grams) all-purpose flour

1. **TO MAKE THE DOUGH:** Place the butter in the work bowl of a food processor fitted with the metal blade and process, scraping down the sides of the bowl as needed, until creamy. Add the confectioners' sugar and process to blend well. Add the ground almonds, salt, and vanilla and continue to process until smooth, scraping the bowl as necessary. Lightly stir the eggs together with a fork and, with the machine running, add them to the work bowl; process for a few seconds to blend. Finally, add the flour and pulse until the mixture just starts to come together. When the dough forms moist curds and clumps and then starts to form a ball, stop!—you don't want to overwork it. The dough will be very soft, and that's just as it should be. (If you want to make the dough in a mixer, use the paddle attachment. First beat the butter until it is smooth, then add the remaining ingredients in the order given above. Just be careful when you add the flour—you must stop mixing as soon as the flour is incorporated.)

2. Gather the dough into a ball and divide it into 3 pieces. Gently press each piece into a disk and wrap each disk in plastic. Allow the dough to rest in the refrigerator for at least 4 hours, or for up to 2 days, before rolling and baking. (*The dough can be wrapped airtight and frozen for up to a month.*)

3. **TO ROLL AND BAKE TART CRUSTS**: For each tart, butter the right-sized tart pan and place it on a parchment-lined baking sheet. If you are making more than one tart, work with one piece of dough at a time.

4. What makes this dough so delicious—lots of butter—also makes it a little difficult to roll. The easiest way to work with *pâte sucrée* is to roll it out between sheets of plastic wrap. Just flatten a large piece of plastic wrap against the counter and roll the dough between that and another piece of plastic. Turn the dough over often so that you can roll it out on both sides, and as you're rolling, make sure to lift the sheets of plastic several times so that they don't crease and get rolled into the dough. (If the dough becomes too soft, just slip it, still between plastic, onto a baking sheet and pop it into the fridge for a few minutes.) Remove one sheet of the plastic and center the dough (exposed side down) over the tart pan. Press the dough against the bottom of the pan and up the sides, remove the top sheet of plastic wrap, and roll your rolling pin across the rim of the pan to cut off the excess. If the dough cracks or splits while you're working, don't worry—you can patch the cracks with leftover dough (moisten the edges to "glue" them into place). Just be careful not to stretch the dough in the pan (what you stretch now will shrink later). Chill for at least 30 minutes in the refrigerator. (Repeat with the remaining dough, if necessary.)

5. When you are ready to bake the crust(s), preheat the oven to 350°F (180°C). Line the crust with a circle of parchment paper or foil and fill with dried beans or rice.

6. Bake the crust (or crusts) for 20 to 25 minutes, or just until very lightly colored. If the crust needs to be fully baked, remove the parchment and beans and bake the crust for another 3 to 5 minutes, or until golden. Transfer to a rack to cool.

KEEPING: Wrapped airtight, the dough can be kept in the refrigerator for up to 2 days or frozen for a month. Frozen disks of dough take 45 to 60 minutes at average room temperature to reach a good rolling-out consistency. Baked crusts can be kept uncovered at room temperature for about 8 hours.

Inside-Out Puff Pastry /

Pâte Feuilletée Inversée

The first time I heard about making puff pastry with this unusual inside-out method was from Pierre Hermé (see page 56). And while my American baking friends and I were surprised by the method, Pierre was quick to say that he hadn't invented it. In fact, although it's rarely seen here in the States and is not all that common among Paris pâtissiers (although the best ones, including Stéphane Vandermeersch (see page 162), who has won accolades for his puff-pastry–based desserts, do, in fact, make this reverse dough), it is an old recipe. I guess we can say that Pierre resurrected it. And, if that's the case, we can all thank him, because not only does inside-out puff pastry produce a glorious dough, one that rises magnificently and is both melt-in-your-mouth tender and irresistibly crackly, but it is easier to work with and faster to make than what we know as traditional puff pastry.

All puff pastry is made with two doughs, one encasing the other. In the traditional recipe, the inner dough is almost all butter and the outer dough is only slightly buttery. In reverse puff pastry, the proportions are turned around, so that the outer dough gets the heartier share of butter. All puff pastry is given six "turns," that is, it is rolled out, then folded over on itself six times. It is this rolling and folding that creates the pastry's thousand layers of butter and dough and makes puffing possible. With traditional puff pastry, each roll-out and fold-over must be accomplished singly, with chilling time between each turn. But because reverse puff pastry is sturdier than the traditional dough, it can be given double turns, cutting the roll-out time almost in half.

THE FIRST DOUGH

3½ sticks (14 ounces; 400 grams) unsalted butter, at room temperature

1¼ cups (175 grams) all-purpose flour

1. **TO MAKE THE FIRST DOUGH:** Put the butter in a mixer fitted with the paddle attachment and beat just until it is smooth. Add the flour and mix only until you have clumps. Use a spatula to mix any flour that is left on the bottom of the bowl into the butter, then turn the dough out onto a large sheet of plastic wrap. Flatten the dough into a 6-inch (15-cm) square, wrap it well, and refrigerate it for at least 2 hours.

2. **TO MAKE THE SECOND DOUGH:** Mix together the water, salt, and vinegar; keep nearby. Put 3 cups flour in the mixer bowl and, working on medium-low speed, still with the paddle attachment, add the melted butter, mixing until the flour is moistened. At this point, you'll have a lumpy dough. Still mixing on medium-low speed, begin to pour the water very slowly down the side of the bowl. Keep mixing, scraping down the bowl and adding water, until you have a soft, elastic dough that cleans the sides of the bowl. You may not need all the water. Or, if the dough doesn't come together, it may need up to a tablespoon more flour or a tablespoon or two more water. Scrape the dough onto a sheet of plastic wrap, shape it into a square that is 1 to 2 inches (2.5 to 5 cm) smaller than the butter-flour square, wrap it well, and chill it for at least 2 hours.

3. **TO ROLL AND TURN THE DOUGH:** Place the first dough on a very well-floured work surface (marble is ideal) and dust the top with flour. Press your rolling pin against the dough to produce a series of parallel indentations, which will soften the dough and help you roll it at the start. Rolling in all directions and on both sides, and making sure to lift and turn the dough often as you roll, roll the dough into a 12 x 7-inch (30 x 18-cm) rectangle. Position the chilled second dough on the bottom half of the rolled-out dough. Fold the top half of the rolled-out dough over it and press to form a sealed package. It is important that the second dough reaches into the corners of the square, so push the dough into the corners with your fingertips if needed. Square the bundle (which will probably be about 7 to 8 inches [18 to 20 cm] on a side) by tapping the rolling pin against the sides. Wrap the dough in plastic and refrigerate for at least 1 hour.

4. To make the first double turn, place the dough on a well-floured work surface and dust the top with flour. Again, rolling in all directions and on both sides, taking care not to roll over the edges and keeping the work surface and the dough as well floured as needed, roll the dough until it is about three times longer than it is wide, about 7 to 8 inches (18 to 20 cm) wide and about 21 to 24 inches (52 to 60 cm) long. (It's not crucial that your dough be the specified measurements. What's important is to roll the dough to three times its width, whatever its width.) If the dough cracks while you're rolling, patch it as best you can and keep going. To perform the double (or wallet) turn, fold the bottom quarter of the dough up to the center of the dough, then fold the top quarter of the dough down to the center. Now fold the dough in half at the center. You'll have four layers of dough. Brush off any excess flour, wrap the dough well, and chill it again for at least 1 hour.

THE SECOND DOUGH

¾ cup (185 grams) water, or as needed

2 teaspoons salt

¼ teaspoon white vinegar

About 3 cups (420 grams) all-purpose flour

1 stick (4 ounces; 115 grams) unsalted butter, melted and cooled

5. For the second double turn, position the dough so that the closed fold, the one that looks like the spine of a book, is to your left, and repeat the rolling and folding process as above. Brush off the excess flour, wrap the dough in plastic, and chill it again for about 1 hour. *(The dough can be made to this point and kept refrigerated for up to 48 hours. In fact, at this point, it is good to give the dough a rest of more than 3 hours.)*

6. On the day you need the dough, give it its last turn, a single turn. Position the dough with the closed fold to your left and roll the dough out as before. Now fold the dough like a business letter: Fold the bottom third of the dough up so that it covers the middle third of the dough and then fold the top third over so that it meets the bottom of the folded dough. (If your dough was three times longer than it was wide, this fold will result in a square; if not, it will still be fine.) Brush off any excess flour, wrap the dough well, and chill it for at least 30 minutes before using it in any recipe. If you have time, chill the dough longer; then, after you've rolled the dough out for your recipe, let the rolled-out dough chill for 30 minutes more before cutting and baking. The best plan is to roll the dough out, transfer it to a baking sheet, cover, and chill it on the baking sheet, then, with the chilled dough still on the sheet, do the actual cutting.

KEEPING: This dough can be refrigerated for a total of 3 days from the time you make the two base doughs to the time you use the puff pastry for a dessert. Once the dough is made, it can be divided into portions, wrapped airtight, and kept in the freezer for up to 1 month. Thaw, still wrapped, in the refrigerator overnight before rolling it out to cut and bake.

Source Guide

CHOCOLATES

For retail sources and a catalogue for Valrhona Chocolates, contact:
Valrhona Inc.
1801 Avenue of the Stars,
Suite 829
Los Angeles, CA 90067
310-277-0401

For retail sources or on-line orders for Scharffen Berger Chocolates contact:
www.scharffenberger.com

For bulk chocolate (as well as baking equipment):
New York Cake & Baking Distributors
56 West 22nd Street
New York, NY 10010
212-675-2253

FLEUR DE SEL

Dean & DeLuca
560 Broadway
New York, NY 10012
212-226-6800
www.deananddeluca.com

King Arthur Flour Company
The Baker's Catalogue
P.O. Box 876
Norwich, VT 05055
800-827-6836
www.kingarthurflour.com

All Sutton Place Gourmet stores, Balducci's, and Hay Day markets
800-3-GOURMET

FRUIT PURÉES

The Perfect Purée of Napa Valley
975 Vintage Avenue, Suite B
St. Helena, CA 94574
800-556-3707
www.perfectpuree.com

READY-MADE ALL-BUTTER PUFF PASTRY

Dufour Pastry Kitchens
25 Ninth Avenue
New York, NY 10014
212-929-2800

All Sutton Place Gourmet stores, Balducci's, and Hay Day markets
800-3-GOURMET

TEAS FROM FAUCHON

Fauchon
442 Park Avenue
New York, NY 10022
212-308-5919

575 Madison Avenue
New York, NY 10022
212-605-0130

TEAS FROM MARIAGE FRÈRES

www.mariagefreres.com

All Williams-Sonoma stores
www.williams-sonoma.com

Dean & DeLuca
560 Broadway
New York, NY 10012
212-226-6800
www.deananddeluca.com

All Sutton Place Gourmet stores, Balducci's, and Hay Day markets
800-3-GOURMET

Les Bonnes Adresses

Where to Find the Pâtisseries, Boulangeries, and *Salons de Thé* in *Paris Sweets*

CHRISTIAN CONSTANT
37 rue d'Assas
75007 Paris
(0) 1–53–63–15–15

30 boulevard Haussmann
75008 Paris
(0) 1–47–70–05–25

DALLOYAU
101 rue du Faubourg Saint-Honoré
75008 Paris
(0) 1–42–99–90–00

25 boulevard des Capucines
75002 Paris
(0) 1–47–03–47–00

5 boulevard Beaumarchais
75004 Paris
(0) 1–48–87–89–88

2 place Edmond Rostand
75006 Paris
(0) 1–43–39–31–10

69 rue de la Convention
75015 Paris
(0) 1–45–77–64–27

63 rue de Grenelle
75007 Paris
(0) 1–45–49–95–30

At Lafayette Gourmet
48–52 boulevard Haussmann
75009 Paris
(0) 1–53–20–05–00

FAUCHON
26 place de la Madeleine
75008 Paris
(0) 1–47–42–60–11

442 Park Avenue
New York, NY 10022
212-308-5919

575 Madison Avenue
New York, NY 10022
212-605-0130

**MAISON KAYSER (SOME SHOPS ARE
CALLED BOULANGERIE KAYSER)**
8 rue Monge
75005 Paris
(0) 1–44–07–01–42

14 rue Monge
75005 Paris
(0) 1-44-07-17-81

87 rue d'Assas
75005 Paris
(0) 1–43–54–92–31

49 rue Linois
75015 Paris
(0) 1–45–75–41–85

79 rue du Commerce
75015 Paris
(0) 1–44–19–88–54

LADURÉE
16 rue Royale
75008 Paris
(0) 1–42–60–21–79

75 avenue des Champs-Élysées
75008 Paris
(0) 1–40–75–08–75

Au Grand Magasin du
Printemps
62 boulevard Haussmann
75009 Paris
(0) 1–42–82–40–10

21 rue Bonaparte
75006 Paris
(0) 1–44–07–64–87

PÂTISSERIE ARNAUD LARHER
53 rue Caulaincourt
75018 Paris
(0) 1–42–57–68–08

LENÔTRE
48 avenue Victor-Hugo
75016 Paris
(0) 1–45–02–21–21

15 boulevard Courcelles
75008 Paris
(0) 1–45–63–87–63

61 rue Lecourbe
75015 Paris
(0) 1–42–73–20–97

44 rue Auteuil
75016 Paris
(0) 1–45–24–52–52

121 avenue de Wagram
75017 Paris
(0) 1–47–63–70–30

PÂTISSERIE LERCH
4 rue du Cardinal Lemoine
75005 Paris
(0) 1–43–26–15–80

LA MAISON DU CHOCOLAT

225 rue du Faubourg-Saint-Honoré
75008 Paris
(0) 1–42–27–39–44

52 rue Francois 1er
75008 Paris
(0) 1–47–23–38–25

8 boulevard de la Madeleine
75008 Paris
(0) 1–47–42–86–52

19 rue de Sèvres
75006 Paris
(0) 1–45–44–20–40

30 Rockefeller Plaza
New York, NY 10112
212-265-9404

1018 Madison Avenue
New York, NY 10012
212-744-7117

MARIAGE FRÈRES

30 et 35 rue du Bourg-Tibourg
75004 Paris
(0) 1–42–72–28–11

13 rue des Grands-Augustins
75006 Paris
(0) 1–40–51–82–50

260 rue du Faubourg Saint-Honoré
75008 Paris
(0) 1–46–22–18–54

PÂTISSERIE MULOT

76 rue de Seine
75006 Paris
(0) 1–43–26–85–77

PIERRE HERMÉ PARIS

72 rue Bonaparte
75006 Paris
(0) 1–43–54–47–77

At Rendez-vous
33 rue Marbeuf
75008 Paris
(open 2003)

BOULANGERIE POILÂNE

8 rue du Cherche-Midi
75006 Paris
(0) 1–45–48–42–59

49 boulevard de Grenelle
75015 Paris
(0) 1–45–79–11–49

BOULANGERIE-PÂTISSERIE POUJAURAN

20 rue Jean-Nicot
75007 Paris
(0) 1–47–05–80–88

ROLLET-PRADIER

6 rue de Bourgogne
75007 Paris
(0) 1–45–51–78–36

PÂTISSERIE STOHRER

51 rue Montorgueil
75002 Paris
(0) 1–42–33–38–20

PÂTISSERIE STÉPHANE VANDER-MEERSCH

278 avenue Daumesnil
75012 Paris
(0) 1–43–47–21–66

Index